Pies

pil

Publications International, Ltd.

Pictured on the front cover: Pressure Cooker Peanut Butter Pie *(page 50).*

Pictured on the back cover *(clockwise from bottom):* Chocolate Chess Pie *(page 98),* Taco Pot Pie *(page 174),* Double Blueberry Pie *(page 26)* and Fresh Fruit Tart *(page 126).*

ISBN: 978-1-63938-607-9

Manufactured in China.

8 7 6 5 4 3 2 1

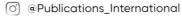

Let's get social!
@Publications_International
@PublicationsInternational
www.pilbooks.com

Contents

Fruit Pies

Classic Apple Pie
makes 8 servings

1 package (14 ounces) refrigerated pie crusts (2 crusts)

6 cups sliced Granny Smith, Crispin or other firm-fleshed apples (about 6 medium)

½ cup sugar

1 tablespoon cornstarch

2 teaspoons lemon juice

½ teaspoon ground cinnamon

½ teaspoon vanilla

⅛ teaspoon salt

⅛ teaspoon ground nutmeg

⅛ teaspoon ground cloves

1 tablespoon whipping cream

1. Let one crust stand at room temperature 15 minutes. Preheat oven to 350°F. Line 9-inch pie plate with crust.

2. Combine apples, sugar, cornstarch, lemon juice, cinnamon, vanilla, salt, nutmeg and cloves in large bowl; toss to coat. Pour into crust.

3. Place second crust over apples; crimp edge to seal. Cut four slits in top crust; brush with cream.

4. Bake 40 minutes or until crust is golden brown. Cool completely on wire rack.

Deep-Dish Blueberry Pie

makes 8 servings

Double-Crust Pie Dough (page 7)

6 **cups fresh blueberries or 2 (16-ounce) packages frozen blueberries, thawed and drained**

2 **tablespoons lemon juice**

1¼ **cups sugar**

3 **tablespoons quick-cooking tapioca**

¼ **teaspoon ground cinnamon**

1 **tablespoon butter, cut into small pieces**

1 Prepare Double-Crust Pie Dough. Preheat oven to 400°F.

2 Place blueberries in large bowl; sprinkle with lemon juice. Combine sugar, tapioca and cinnamon in small bowl; mix well. Add to blueberries; stir gently to blend.

3 Roll out one disc of dough into 12-inch circle on lightly floured surface. Line 9-inch deep-dish pie plate with dough; trim all but ½ inch of overhang. Pour blueberry mixture into crust; dot with butter.

4 Roll out remaining disc of dough into 10-inch circle. Cut four or five shapes from dough with small cookie cutter or knife. Place dough over fruit; trim edge, leaving 1-inch border. Fold excess dough under and even with edge of pie plate. Crimp edge with fork.

5 Bake 15 minutes. *Reduce oven temperature to 350°F.* Bake 40 minutes or until crust is golden brown. Cool on wire rack 30 minutes.

Double-Crust Pie Dough
makes dough for 1 pie

2½ cups all-purpose flour
1 teaspoon salt
1 teaspoon sugar
1 cup (2 sticks) cold butter, cubed
⅓ cup ice water

1 Combine flour, salt and sugar in large bowl. Cut in butter with pastry blender until mixture resembles coarse crumbs.

2 Drizzle water over flour mixture, 2 tablespoons at a time, stirring just until dough comes together. Divide dough in half. Shape each half into a disc; wrap in plastic wrap. Refrigerate at least 30 minutes or up to 2 days.

Lattice-Topped Cherry Pie

makes 8 servings

**Double-Crust Pie Dough
(page 7)**

6 **cups pitted sweet
Bing cherries**

¾ **cup plus 1 tablespoon
granulated sugar,
divided**

3 **tablespoons plus
1 teaspoon cornstarch**

2 **tablespoons lemon juice**

1 **tablespoon half-and-half
or whipping cream**

Granulated sugar

1 Prepare Double-Crust Pie Dough. Preheat oven to 400°F.

2 Combine cherries, ¾ cup sugar, cornstarch and lemon juice in large bowl; toss to coat. Let stand 15 minutes or until syrup forms.

3 Roll out one disc of dough into 12- to 13-inch circle (⅛ to ¼ inch thick) on floured surface. Line 9-inch pie plate with dough, letting excess drape over edge.

4 Roll out remaining disc of dough into 11-inch circle; cut into 12 to 14 strips about ½ inch wide.

5 Pour cherry mixture into crust. Arrange dough strips in lattice design over fruit. Tuck ends of strips under edge of bottom crust; seal edge. Brush dough with half-and-half; sprinkle with remaining 1 tablespoon sugar. Cover loosely with foil.

6 Bake 30 minutes. Remove foil; bake 30 minutes or until filling is thick and bubbly and crust is golden brown. Cool on wire rack.

Cheddar Apple Pie

makes 8 servings

Single-Crust Pie Dough
(page 11)

Streusel (recipe follows)

8 cups sliced peeled apples
(Rome Beauty, Fuji
or Northern Spy)

½ cup packed dark brown
sugar

⅓ cup granulated sugar

3 tablespoons all-purpose
flour

½ teaspoon ground
cinnamon

¼ teaspoon salt

1 cup (4 ounces) shredded
sharp Cheddar cheese,
divided

1 Prepare Single-Crust Pie Dough and Streusel.
Preheat oven to 425°F.

2 Combine apples, brown sugar, granulated sugar,
flour, cinnamon and salt in large bowl; toss to coat.

3 Roll out dough into 11-inch circle on floured surface.
Sprinkle with ½ cup cheese; roll lightly to adhere.
Line 9-inch pie plate with dough; flute edge.

4 Pour apple mixture into crust; pack down fruit.
Sprinkle with Streusel. Place pie on baking sheet.

5 Bake 15 minutes. *Reduce oven temperature to 350°F.*
Cover loosely with foil; bake 35 minutes. Remove
foil; sprinkle pie with remaining ½ cup cheese.
Bake 10 minutes or until cheese is melted and
crust is golden brown. Cool at least 30 minutes
before slicing.

Streusel: Combine ⅓ cup all-purpose flour,
⅓ cup granulated sugar, ⅓ cup packed dark brown
sugar and ¼ teaspoon salt in medium bowl. Cut
in 5 tablespoons cubed butter with pastry blender
until mixture resembles coarse crumbs.

Single-Crust Pie Dough
makes dough for 1 pie

1¼ cups all-purpose flour

½ teaspoon salt

3 tablespoons cold
    shortening, cubed

3 tablespoons cold butter,
    cubed

3 to 4 tablespoons
    ice water

½ teaspoon cider vinegar

1 Combine flour and salt in medium bowl. Cut in
shortening and butter with pastry blender or two
knives until mixture resembles coarse crumbs.
Combine 3 tablespoons water and vinegar in small
bowl. Add to flour mixture; mix with fork until
dough forms, adding additional water as needed.

2 Shape dough into a disc; wrap in plastic wrap.
Refrigerate 30 minutes.

Deep-Dish Streusel Peach Pie

makes about 6 servings

1 can (29 ounces) *or* 2 cans
  (16 ounces each) cling
  peach slices in syrup
⅓ cup plus 1 tablespoon
  granulated sugar,
  divided
1 tablespoon cornstarch
½ teaspoon vanilla
2 cups all-purpose flour,
  divided
½ cup packed brown sugar
⅓ cup quick oats
¼ cup (½ stick) butter,
  melted
½ teaspoon ground
  cinnamon
½ teaspoon salt
½ cup cold shortening,
  cubed
4 to 5 tablespoons
  cold water

1 Drain peaches, reserving ¾ cup syrup. Combine ⅓ cup granulated sugar and cornstarch in small saucepan. Gradually stir in reserved syrup until well blended. Cook and stir over low heat until thickened. Remove from heat; stir in vanilla.

2 Combine ½ cup flour, brown sugar, oats, butter and cinnamon in small bowl; stir until mixture resembles coarse crumbs.

3 Preheat oven to 350°F. Combine remaining 1½ cups flour, 1 tablespoon granulated sugar and salt in small bowl. Cut in shortening with pastry blender until mixture resembles coarse crumbs. Sprinkle water, 1 tablespoon at a time, over flour mixture; stir with fork until mixture holds together. Shape dough into a ball; flatten into 5- to 6-inch disc.

4 Roll out dough into ⅛-inch-thick square on lightly floured surface. Cut into 10-inch square.

5 Press dough into bottom and 1 inch up sides of 8-inch square baking dish. Spread peaches over crust. Pour sauce over peaches; sprinkle with crumb topping.

6 Bake 45 minutes. Remove to wire rack to cool slightly. Serve pie warm or at room temperature.

Rhubarb Cherry Pie

makes 8 servings

Double-Crust Pie Dough (page 7)

4 cups sliced (½-inch slices) fresh rhubarb (about 1¼ pounds)

1½ cups fresh or frozen Bing cherries, pitted and cut into halves

1 cup sugar

2 tablespoons cornstarch

½ teaspoon ground cinnamon

⅛ teaspoon salt

2 tablespoons butter, cut into small pieces

1 Prepare Double-Crust Pie Dough. Preheat oven to 400°F.

2 Combine rhubarb and cherries in large bowl. Combine sugar, cornstarch, cinnamon and salt in small bowl; mix well. Add to rhubarb mixture; toss to coat.

3 Roll out one disc of dough into 12-inch circle on floured surface. Line 9-inch pie plate with dough, allowing excess dough to hang over edge.

4 Roll out remaining disc of dough into 11-inch circle. Cut into strips about ¾ inch wide.

5 Pour fruit mixture into crust; dot with butter. Arrange dough strips in lattice design over fruit. Tuck ends of strips under edge of bottom crust, pressing to seal. Flute edge.

6 Bake about 45 minutes or until rhubarb is tender and juices are bubbly, covering pie loosely with foil during last 10 minutes to prevent overbrowning. Cool on wire rack. Serve warm or at room temperature.

Note: The pie can also be made using frozen sliced rhubarb. Bake in a preheated oven for 50 to 55 minutes or until the fruit is soft and the juices are bubbly, covering loosely with foil during the last 15 minutes of baking to prevent overbrowning.

Cranberry Apple Nut Pie

makes 8 servings

Double-Crust Pie Dough (page 7)

1 cup sugar

3 tablespoons all-purpose flour

¼ teaspoon salt

4 cups sliced peeled tart apples (4 large apples)

2 cups fresh cranberries

½ cup golden raisins

½ cup coarsely chopped pecans

1 tablespoon grated lemon peel

2 tablespoons butter, cut into small pieces

1 egg, beaten

1 Prepare Double-Crust Pie Dough. Preheat oven to 425°F.

2 Roll out one disc of dough into 11-inch circle on floured surface. Line 9-inch pie plate with dough.

3 Combine sugar, flour and salt in large bowl; mix well. Add apples, cranberries, raisins, pecans and lemon peel; toss to coat. Pour into crust; dot with butter.

4 Roll out remaining disc of dough into 11-inch circle; place over fruit. Trim excess dough; seal and flute edge. Cut three slits in center of top crust. Brush top crust with beaten egg.

5 Bake 35 minutes or until apples are tender when pierced with fork and crust is golden brown. Cool on wire rack 15 minutes. Serve warm or cool completely.

Plum Walnut Pie

makes 8 servings

Single-Crust Pie Dough
(page 11)

Oat Streusel
(recipe follows)

8 cups thinly sliced plums

⅓ cup granulated sugar

⅓ cup packed brown sugar

3 to 4 tablespoons
all-purpose flour

1 tablespoon honey

½ teaspoon ground
cinnamon

¼ teaspoon ground ginger

⅛ teaspoon salt

½ cup candied walnuts

1 Prepare Single-Crust Pie Dough and Oat Streusel. Preheat oven to 425°F.

2 Combine plums, granulated sugar, brown sugar, 3 tablespoons flour (use 4 tablespoons if plums are very juicy), honey, cinnamon, ginger and salt in large bowl; toss to coat.

3 Roll out dough into 11-inch circle on floured surface. Line 9-inch pie plate with dough; flute edge.

4 Pour plum mixture into crust; sprinkle with streusel. Place pie on baking sheet.

5 Bake 15 minutes. *Reduce oven temperature to 350°F.* Sprinkle pie with walnuts. Bake 30 minutes. Loosely tent pie with foil; bake 30 minutes or until filling is bubbly and crust is golden brown. Let stand at least 30 minutes before slicing.

> **Oat Streusel:** Combine ¼ cup all-purpose flour, ¼ cup old-fahioned oats, ¼ cup granulated sugar, ¼ cup packed light brown sugar and ⅛ teaspoon salt in medium bowl. Add ¼ cup (½ stick) cubed butter; crumble with fingertips until mixture resembles coarse crumbs.

Spiced Peach Pie

makes 8 servings

Double-Crust Pie Dough (page 7)

1 egg, separated

2 tablespoons cornstarch

2 teaspoons ground cinnamon

½ teaspoon ground nutmeg

⅛ teaspoon salt

½ cup unsweetened apple juice concentrate

1 teaspoon vanilla

5 cups sliced peeled fresh peaches or frozen unsweetened sliced peaches, thawed and well drained

1 tablespoon butter, cut into small pieces

1 teaspoon cold water

1 Prepare Double-Crust Pie Dough. Preheat oven to 400°F.

2 Roll out one disc of dough into 11-inch circle on floured surface. Line 9-inch pie plate with dough. Beat egg white in small bowl until frothy; brush over dough.

3 Combine cornstarch, cinnamon, nutmeg and salt in large bowl; mix well. Stir in apple juice concentrate and vanilla. Add peaches; toss gently to coat. Pour into crust; dot with butter.

4 Roll out remaining disc of dough into 10-inch circle; cut into ½-inch-wide strips. Arrange in lattice design over fruit. Seal and flute edge. Beat egg yolk and water in small bowl; brush over dough.

5 Bake 50 minutes or until crust is golden brown and filling is thick and bubbly.* Cool on wire rack. Serve warm or at room temperature.

Cover pie loosely with foil after 30 minutes to prevent overbrowning, if necessary.

Apple-Pear Praline Pie

makes 8 servings

Double-Crust Pie Dough (page 7)

4 cups sliced peeled Granny Smith apples

2 cups sliced peeled pears

¾ cup granulated sugar

¼ cup plus 1 tablespoon all-purpose flour, divided

4 teaspoons ground cinnamon

¼ teaspoon salt

½ cup (1 stick) plus 2 tablespoons butter, divided

1 cup packed brown sugar

1 tablespoon half-and-half or milk

1 cup chopped pecans

1 Prepare Double-Crust Pie Dough.

2 Combine apples, pears, granulated sugar, ¼ cup flour, cinnamon and salt in large bowl; toss to coat. Let stand 15 minutes.

3 Preheat oven to 350°F. Roll out one disc of dough into 11-inch circle on floured surface. Line 9-inch deep-dish pie plate with dough; sprinkle with remaining 1 tablespoon flour.

4 Pour fruit mixture into crust; dot with 2 tablespoons butter. Roll out remaining disc of dough into 10-inch circle. Place over fruit; seal and flute edge. Cut several slits in top crust.

5 Bake 1 hour. Meanwhile, combine remaining ½ cup butter, brown sugar and half-and-half in small saucepan; bring to a boil over medium heat, stirring frequently. Boil 2 minutes, stirring constantly. Remove from heat; stir in pecans. Spread over pie.

6 Cool pie on wire rack 15 minutes. Serve warm or at room temperature.

Peach Cherry Pie

makes 8 servings

1 refrigerated pie crust
(half of 14-ounce
package)
  Cinnamon Streusel
Topping (recipe
follows)
¾ cup granulated sugar
3 tablespoons quick-
cooking tapioca
1 teaspoon grated
lemon peel
½ teaspoon ground
cinnamon
⅛ teaspoon salt
4 cups peach slices
(about 7 medium)
2 cups Bing cherries, pitted
1 tablespoon lemon juice
2 tablespoons butter,
cut into small pieces
  Vanilla ice cream
(optional)

1 Let crust stand at room temperature 15 minutes.
Preheat oven to 375°F.

2 Prepare Streusel Topping. Line 9-inch pie plate
with crust; flute edge.

3 Combine granulated sugar, tapioca, lemon peel,
cinnamon and salt in large bowl; mix well. Add
peaches, cherries and lemon juice; toss to coat.
Pour into crust; dot with butter. Sprinkle with
topping.

4 Bake 40 minutes or until filling is bubbly and crust
is golden brown. Cool on wire rack 15 minutes.
Serve warm or at room temperature with ice
cream, if desired.

> **Cinnamon Streusel Topping:** Combine
> ¾ cup old-fashioned oats, ⅓ cup all-purpose flour,
> ⅓ cup packed brown sugar and ¾ teaspoon ground
> cinnamon in medium bowl. Stir in ¼ cup (½ stick)
> melted butter until mixture resembles coarse
> crumbs.

Double Blueberry Pie

makes 8 servings

Cream Cheese Pie Dough
(recipe follows)

2 pints (4 cups) fresh
   or thawed frozen
   blueberries

2 tablespoons cornstarch

⅔ cup no-sugar-added
   blueberry preserves,
   melted

¼ teaspoon ground nutmeg

1 egg yolk

1 tablespoon sour cream

1 Prepare Cream Cheese Pie Dough. Preheat oven to 425°F.

2 Roll out one disc of dough into 11-inch circle on floured surface. Line 9-inch pie plate with dough.

3 Combine blueberries and cornstarch in medium bowl; toss gently to coat. Gently stir in preserves and nutmeg. Pour into crust.

4 Roll out remaining disc of dough into 11-inch circle; place over fruit. Turn edge under; seal and flute. Cut several slits or circle in center of top crust.

5 Bake 10 minutes. *Reduce oven temperature to 350°F.* Beat egg yolk and sour cream in small bowl; brush lightly over crust. Bake 40 minutes or until crust is golden brown. Cool on wire rack 15 minutes. Serve warm, at room temperature or chilled.

Cream Cheese Pie Dough

makes dough for 1 pie

1½ cups all-purpose flour

½ cup (1 stick) cold butter,
   cubed

3 ounces cold cream
   cheese, cubed

1 teaspoon vanilla

1 Place flour in large bowl. Cut in butter with pastry blender until mixture resembles coarse crumbs. Blend in cream cheese and vanilla until mixture forms dough.

2 Divide dough in half. Shape each half into a disc; wrap in plastic wrap. Refrigerate 30 minutes.

Apple Crunch Pie

makes 8 servings

1 refrigerated pie crust (half of 14-ounce package)

¾ cup all-purpose flour, divided

¼ cup packed brown sugar

¼ cup chopped walnuts

4 tablespoons (½ stick) butter, melted, divided

1¼ teaspoons ground cinnamon, divided

¾ teaspoon ground nutmeg, divided

1 cup granulated sugar

½ teaspoon ground ginger

¼ teaspoon salt

4 cups diced peeled apples

1 Let crust stand at room temperature 15 minutes. Preheat oven to 350°F.

2 Line 9-inch pie plate with crust; flute or crimp edge.

3 Combine ½ cup flour, brown sugar, walnuts, 2 tablespoons butter, ¼ teaspoon cinnamon and ¼ teaspoon nutmeg in small bowl; mix well. Spread in single layer on baking sheet. Bake 20 minutes on lowest rack of oven.

4 Combine remaining ¼ cup flour, 2 tablespoons butter, 1 teaspoon cinnamon, ½ teaspoon nutmeg, granulated sugar, ginger and salt in large bowl; mix well. Add apples; toss to coat. Pour into crust.

5 Bake 20 minutes on top rack of oven. Remove baking sheet from oven; let stand 5 minutes or until topping is cool enough to handle. Crumble over apple mixture.

6 Bake 25 to 35 minutes or until apples are tender and crust is golden brown. Cool completely on wire rack.

Strawberry Rhubarb Pie

makes 8 servings

Double-Crust Pie Dough (page 7)

1½ **cups granulated sugar**

½ **cup cornstarch**

2 **tablespoons quick-cooking tapioca**

1 **tablespoon grated lemon peel**

¼ **teaspoon ground allspice**

4 **cups sliced rhubarb (1-inch pieces)**

3 **cups sliced fresh strawberries**

1 **egg, beaten**

Coarse sugar (optional)

1 Prepare Double-Crust Pie Dough. Preheat oven to 425°F.

2 Roll out one disc of dough into 11-inch circle on floured surface. Line 9-inch pie plate with dough.

3 Combine granulated sugar, cornstarch, tapioca, lemon peel and allspice in large bowl; mix well. Add rhubarb and strawberries; toss gently to coat. Pour into crust.

4 Roll out remaining disc of dough into 10-inch circle; cut into ½-inch-wide strips. Arrange in lattice design over filling. Seal and flute edge. Brush dough with beaten egg; sprinkle with coarse sugar, if desired.

5 Bake 50 minutes or until filling is thick and bubbly and crust is golden brown. Cool on wire rack. Serve warm or at room temperature.

Peach Raspberry Pie

makes 8 servings

Single-Crust Pie Dough
(page 11)

Almond Crumb Topping
(recipe follows)

5 cups sliced peeled
peaches (about
2 pounds)

2 tablespoons lemon juice

1 cup fresh raspberries

½ cup sugar

2 tablespoons quick-
cooking tapioca

½ teaspoon ground
cinnamon

¼ teaspoon ground nutmeg

1 Prepare Single-Crust Pie Dough and Almond Crumb Topping. Preheat oven to 400°F.

2 Roll out dough into 12-inch circle on floured surface. Line 9-inch pie plate with dough; flute edge. Refrigerate 15 minutes.

3 Place peaches in large bowl. Sprinkle with lemon juice; toss to coat. Gently stir in raspberries.

4 Combine sugar, tapioca, cinnamon and nutmeg in small bowl. Sprinkle over fruit mixture; toss to coat. Pour into crust; sprinkle with crumb topping.

5 Bake 15 minutes. *Reduce oven temperature to 350°F.* Bake 30 minutes or until filling is bubbly. Cool on wire rack 15 minutes. Serve warm or at room temperature.

Almond Crumb Topping: Combine ⅔ cup old-fashioned or quick oats, ¼ cup all-purpose flour, ¼ cup packed brown sugar, ¼ cup slivered almonds and ½ teaspoon ground cinnamon in medium bowl. Blend in 3 tablespoons softened butter until mixture resembles coarse crumbs.

Tip: To substitute frozen fruit, thaw 5 cups frozen peach slices in a large bowl for 1½ to 2 hours. Continue with step 3, using frozen raspberries (do not thaw). Bake as directed in step 5.

Country Apple Pie

makes 8 servings

2⅓ cups all-purpose flour, divided

¾ cup plus 1 tablespoon sugar, divided

½ teaspoon baking powder

½ teaspoon salt

¾ cup (1½ sticks) plus 3 tablespoons cold butter, cubed, divided

4 to 5 tablespoons ice water

1 egg, separated

7 medium Jonathan or Granny Smith apples, peeled and sliced

1 tablespoon lemon juice

1¼ teaspoons ground cinnamon

1 tablespoon sour cream

1 Combine 2 cups flour, 1 tablespoon sugar, baking powder and salt in large bowl. Cut in ¾ cup butter with pastry blender until mixture resembles coarse crumbs. Add water, 1 tablespoon at a time; stir with fork until mixture holds together. Shape dough into two discs. Wrap in plastic wrap; refrigerate 30 minutes or until firm.

2 Roll out one disc of dough into 12-inch circle (about ⅛ inch thick) on lightly floured surface with lightly floured rolling pin. Gently line 9-inch glass pie plate with dough. (Do not stretch dough.) Trim dough, leaving ½-inch overhang. Brush with egg white.

3 Preheat oven to 450°F. Place apples in large bowl; sprinkle with lemon juice. Combine remaining ⅓ cup flour, ¾ cup sugar and cinnamon in small bowl; mix well. Add to apples; toss to coat. Pour into crust; dot with remaining 3 tablespoons butter.

4 Moisten edge of dough with water. Roll out remaining disc of dough into 12-inch circle; place over fruit. Fold excess dough under and even with edge of pie plate; flute or crimp edge. Cut four small slits in center of top crust. Beat egg yolk and sour cream in small bowl.

5 Bake pie 10 minutes. *Reduce oven temperature to 375°F.* Bake 35 minutes. Brush crust with egg yolk mixture; bake 20 to 25 minutes or until crust is golden brown. Cool completely on wire rack.

Pantry Pies

All-American Cookie Pie

makes 8 servings

1 refrigerated pie crust (half of 14-ounce package)

¾ cup (1½ sticks) butter, softened

½ cup granulated sugar

½ cup packed brown sugar

½ teaspoon vanilla

2 eggs

¾ cup all-purpose flour

¼ teaspoon salt

1 cup (6 ounces) semisweet chocolate chunks or chips

1 cup chopped nuts

1 Let crust stand at room temperature 15 minutes. Preheat oven to 325°F.

2 Line 9-inch pie plate with crust; flute or crimp edge.

3 Beat butter, granulated sugar, brown sugar and vanilla in large bowl with electric mixer at medium speed about 3 minutes or until light and fluffy. Add eggs; beat until well blended. Beat in flour and salt at low speed just until blended. Stir in chocolate chunks and nuts. Spread evenly in crust.

4 Bake 65 to 70 minutes or until toothpick inserted into center comes out clean. Cool completely on wire rack.

Cinnamon Ginger Pumpkin Pie

makes 8 servings

1 refrigerated pie crust
   (half of 14-ounce
   package)
1 tablespoon sugar
1 tablespoon ground
   cinnamon
2 teaspoons ground ginger
1 teaspoon ground cloves
1 teaspoon ground nutmeg
½ teaspoon salt
3 eggs
2½ teaspoons vanilla
1 can (15 ounces)
   pure pumpkin
⅓ cup sour cream
1 can (14 ounces)
   sweetened condensed
   milk
   Whole pecans (optional)
   Whipped cream
   (optional)

1 Let crust stand at room temperature 15 minutes. Preheat oven to 425°F.

2 Line 9-inch deep-dish pie plate with crust; flute or crimp edge.

3 Whisk sugar, cinnamon, ginger, cloves, nutmeg and salt in large bowl until blended. Whisk in eggs and vanilla until smooth. Add pumpkin and sour cream; whisk until blended. Gradually whisk in sweetened condensed milk until well blended. Pour into crust.

4 Bake 15 minutes. *Reduce oven temperature to 350°F.* Bake 40 to 45 minutes or until knife inserted near center comes out clean. Cool on wire rack at least 1½ hours before serving. Garnish with pecans and whipped cream.

Italian Chocolate Pie

makes 8 servings

¼ cup pine nuts

3 tablespoons packed
   brown sugar

1 tablespoon grated
   orange peel

1 unbaked 9-inch pie crust

4 ounces bittersweet
   chocolate, coarsely
   chopped

3 tablespoons unsalted
   butter

1 can (5 ounces)
   evaporated milk

3 eggs

3 tablespoons hazelnut
   liqueur

1 teaspoon vanilla
   Whipped cream
   Chocolate curls (optional)

1 Toast pine nuts in small skillet over medium heat until golden brown, stirring constantly. Finely chop pine nuts; cool to room temperature.

2 Combine pine nuts, brown sugar and orange peel in small bowl; mix well. Sprinkle over bottom of pie crust; gently press into crust.

3 Preheat oven to 325°F. Combine chocolate and butter in small saucepan; heat over low heat until melted, stirring frequently. Set aside to cool to room temperature.

4 Combine chocolate mixture and evaporated milk in medium bowl; beat with electric mixer at medium speed until blended. Add eggs, one at a time, beating well after each addition. Stir in hazelnut liqueur and vanilla. Pour into crust.

5 Bake on center rack of oven 30 to 40 minutes or until set. Cool completely on wire rack. Refrigerate until ready to serve. Top with whipped cream; garnish with chocolate curls.

Flat Fruit Pie

makes 12 servings

2 packages (8 ounces each) dried mixed fruit (pitted prunes, pears, apples, apricots and peaches)

3 cups water

½ cup sugar

½ teaspoon ground cinnamon

¼ teaspoon ground cloves

Flaky Pie Dough (recipe follows)

1 teaspoon lemon juice

1 Combine dried fruit, 3 cups water, sugar, cinnamon and cloves in medium saucepan; cook over medium heat until sugar is dissolved, stirring occasionally. Reduce heat to low; cover and simmer 45 minutes or until fruit is tender. Meanwhile, prepare Flaky Pie Dough.

2 Transfer fruit to blender or food processor; blend until fruit is coarsely puréed. (Purée should measure 3 cups. If you have more than that amount, cook until reduced to 3 cups, stirring frequently.) Stir in lemon juice. Set aside to cool completely.

3 Preheat oven to 400°F. Roll out one disc of dough into 13-inch circle on floured surface. Transfer to 12-inch pizza pan; trim to leave ½-inch overhang. Spread fruit mixture over dough. Roll out remaining disc of dough into 13-inch circle; place over filling. Cut slits or small shapes in center. Fold edge of top crust under bottom crust; seal and flute.

4 Bake 35 minutes or until crust is golden brown. Cool on wire rack 1 hour.

Flaky Pie Dough

3⅓ cups all-purpose flour

¾ teaspoon salt

1 cup cold shortening or lard, cubed

6 to 8 tablespoons cold water

Combine flour and salt in medium bowl. Cut in shortening with pastry blender until mixture resembles coarse crumbs. Sprinkle with water, 1 tablespoon at a time, stirring until dough forms. Divide dough in half. Shape each half into a disc; wrap in plastic wrap. Refrigerate 30 minutes.

Caribbean Coconut Pie

makes 8 servings

1 frozen 9-inch deep-dish
   pie crust

1 can (14 ounces)
   sweetened condensed
   milk

¾ cup flaked coconut

2 eggs

½ cup hot water

2 teaspoons grated
   lime peel

  Juice of 1 lime

¼ teaspoon salt

⅛ teaspoon ground
   red pepper

  Whipped cream
  (optional)

1 Preheat oven to 400°F. Prick holes in bottom of crust with fork. Bake 10 minutes or until lightly browned. Cool on wire rack 15 minutes.

2 *Reduce oven temperature to 350°F.* Whisk sweetened condensed milk, coconut, eggs, hot water, lime peel, lime juice, salt and red pepper in large bowl until well blended. Pour into crust.

3 Bake 30 minutes or until knife inserted into center comes out clean. Cool completely on wire rack. Serve with whipped cream, if desired.

Pumpkin Pecan Pie

makes 8 servings

1 can (15 ounces)
  pure pumpkin
1 can (14 ounces)
  sweetened condensed
  milk
¼ cup (½ stick) butter,
  softened
2 eggs, divided
1 teaspoon ground
  cinnamon
1 teaspoon vanilla
¼ teaspoon salt
¼ teaspoon ground nutmeg,
  plus additional for
  garnish
1 (6-ounce) graham cracker
  pie crust
2 tablespoons packed
  brown sugar
2 tablespoons dark
  corn syrup
1 tablespoon butter, melted
½ teaspoon maple flavoring
1 cup chopped pecans
  Whipped cream
  (optional)

1 Preheat oven to 400°F.

2 Whisk pumpkin, sweetened condensed milk,
   ¼ cup softened butter, 1 egg, cinnamon, vanilla,
   salt and ¼ teaspoon nutmeg in large bowl until
   well blended. Pour into crust.

3 Bake 20 minutes. Meanwhile, beat remaining
   egg, brown sugar, corn syrup, 1 tablespoon melted
   butter and maple flavoring in medium bowl with
   electric mixer at medium speed until well blended.
   Stir in pecans.

4 Remove pie from oven; top with pecan mixture.
   Reduce oven temperature to 350°F. Bake 25 minutes
   or until knife inserted near center comes out clean.
   Cool completely on wire rack. Top with whipped
   cream and additional nutmeg, if desired.

Southern Oatmeal Pie

makes 8 servings

1 refrigerated pie crust (half of 14-ounce package)

4 eggs

1 cup light corn syrup

½ cup packed brown sugar

6 tablespoons (¾ stick) butter, melted and slightly cooled

1½ teaspoons vanilla

½ teaspoon salt

1 cup quick oats

Whipped cream (optional)

1 Let crust stand at room temperature 15 minutes. Preheat oven to 375°F.

2 Line 9-inch pie plate with crust; flute or crimp edge.

3 Whisk eggs in medium bowl. Whisk in corn syrup, brown sugar, butter, vanilla and salt until well blended. Stir in oats until blended. Pour into crust.

4 Bake 35 minutes or until edge is set. Cool on wire rack. Serve warm or at room temperature with whipped cream, if desired.

Peanut Chocolate Surprise Pie

makes 8 servings

1 cup sugar

½ cup (1 stick) butter, melted

2 eggs

½ cup all-purpose flour

¼ teaspoon salt

½ cup chopped peanuts

½ cup chopped walnuts

½ cup semisweet chocolate chips

¼ cup bourbon

1 teaspoon vanilla

1 frozen 9-inch deep-dish pie crust

Whipped cream (optional)

1 Preheat oven to 350°F.

2 Beat sugar and butter in large bowl with electric mixer at medium speed about 2 minutes or until creamy. Add eggs; beat until well blended. Gradually beat in flour and salt at low speed. Stir in peanuts, walnuts, chocolate chips, bourbon and vanilla until blended. Spread evenly in crust.

3 Bake 40 minutes. Cool on wire rack. Top with whipped cream, if desired.

Pressure Cooker Peanut Butter Pie

makes 8 servings

10 cream-filled chocolate sandwich cookies, crushed into fine crumbs

1½ tablespoons butter, melted

⅔ cup creamy peanut butter

½ cup plus 2 tablespoons whipping cream, divided

2 eggs

⅓ cup whole milk

¼ cup packed brown sugar

½ teaspoon salt

½ teaspoon vanilla

⅓ cup plus ¼ cup semisweet chocolate chips, divided

1½ cups water

2 to 3 tablespoons chopped roasted salted peanuts

1 Spray 7-inch springform pan with nonstick cooking spray. Combine cookie crumbs and butter in small bowl; mix well. Use bottom of glass or measuring cup to press mixture evenly into bottom of prepared pan. Freeze crust 10 minutes while preparing filling.

2 Whisk peanut butter, ½ cup cream, eggs, milk, brown sugar, salt and vanilla in medium bowl until well blended. Sprinkle ⅓ cup chocolate chips over bottom of crust. Pour peanut butter mixture over chocolate chips. Cover pan with foil.

3 Pour water into pressure cooker pot; place rack in pot. Place springform pan on rack. Secure lid and move pressure release valve to sealing or locked position. Cook at high pressure 34 minutes.

4 When cooking is complete, use natural release for 10 minutes, then release remaining pressure. Remove springform pan from pot. Uncover; cool to room temperature. Cover and refrigerate at least 4 hours or overnight.

5 Heat remaining 2 tablespoons cream to a simmer in microwave or in small saucepan over low heat. Add remaining ¼ cup chocolate chips; stir until chocolate is melted and mixture is smooth. Remove side of pan. Sprinkle peanuts over pie; drizzle with chocolate glaze.

Spiced Pumpkin Pie

makes 8 servings

Pie dough for single-crust
9-inch pie (see Tip)

1 can (15 ounces)
pure pumpkin

¾ cup packed brown sugar

2 teaspoons ground
cinnamon

¾ teaspoon ground ginger

½ teaspoon ground nutmeg,
plus additional
for garnish

¼ teaspoon salt

⅛ teaspoon ground cloves

4 eggs, lightly beaten

1 cup light cream or
half-and-half

1 teaspoon vanilla

Whipped cream
(optional)

1 Preheat oven to 400°F.

2 Roll out dough into 13-inch circle on lightly floured surface. Line 9-inch pie plate with dough; flute edge.

3 Whisk pumpkin and brown sugar in large bowl until well blended. Whisk in cinnamon, ginger, ½ teaspoon nutmeg, salt and cloves. Whisk in eggs until blended. Gradually whisk in cream and vanilla until well blended. Pour into crust.

4 Bake 40 to 45 minutes or until knife inserted near center comes out clean. Cool completely on wire rack. Serve warm or at room temperature; garnish with whipped cream and additional nutmeg.

Tip: Use your favorite recipe for pie dough or the Single-Crust Pie Dough on page 11. Or use a refrigerated pie crust (half of a 14-ounce package) or a frozen 9-inch pie crust. Prepare the filling and bake as directed.

Maple Walnut Pie

makes 8 servings

1½ cups all-purpose flour

¾ teaspoon salt, divided

⅓ cup cold shortening, cubed

3 tablespoons cold butter, cubed

4 to 6 tablespoons ice water

3 eggs

1 cup maple syrup

6 tablespoons packed dark brown sugar

3 tablespoons butter, melted

¾ teaspoon vanilla

1½ cups coarsely chopped walnuts

1 Combine 1½ cups flour and ¼ teaspoon salt in medium bowl. Cut in shortening and 3 tablespoons cubed butter with pastry blender until mixture resembles coarse crumbs. Stir in water, 2 tablespoons at a time, with fork until mixture forms dough. Shape dough into a disc; wrap in plastic wrap. Refrigerate 30 minutes.

2 Preheat oven to 425°F. Roll out dough into 11-inch circle on floured surface. Line 9-inch pie plate with dough; flute edge. Place on baking sheet.

3 Bake crust 5 minutes. (It is not necessary to weigh down crust.) *Reduce oven temperature to 350°F.*

4 Beat eggs in large bowl. Whisk in maple syrup, brown sugar, melted butter, vanilla and remaining ½ teaspoon salt until well blended. Stir in walnuts. Pour into crust.

5 Bake 45 minutes or until walnuts are golden brown and filling is slightly puffed. Check pie after 30 minutes and cover loosely with foil, if necessary, to prevent walnuts from burning. Cool on wire rack 30 minutes.

Fruit and Nut Chocolate Chip Pie

makes 8 servings

2 eggs

½ cup packed brown sugar

¼ cup granulated sugar

1 teaspoon vanilla

½ teaspoon grated
   orange peel

⅛ teaspoon salt

1 cup (2 sticks) butter,
   melted and cooled

½ cup all-purpose flour

1 cup semisweet chocolate
   chips

1 cup chopped pecans
   or walnuts

1 cup dried cranberries
   or raisins

1 unbaked 9-inch pie crust

Whipped cream
   (optional)

1 Preheat oven to 325°F.

2 Whisk eggs, brown sugar, granulated sugar, vanilla, orange peel and salt in large bowl until well blended. Whisk in butter and flour until blended. Stir in chocolate chips, pecans and cranberries. Spread evenly in crust.

3 Bake 50 minutes or until top of pie is puffed and golden brown. Cool completely on wire rack. Serve with whipped cream, if desired.

Bourbon Pecan Pie

makes 6 to 8 servings

Pie dough for single-crust
9-inch pie (see Tip)

¼ cup (½ stick) butter,
softened

½ cup sugar

3 eggs

1½ cups light or dark
corn syrup

2 tablespoons bourbon

1 teaspoon vanilla

¼ teaspoon salt

1 cup pecan halves

1 Preheat oven to 350°F. Roll out dough into 12-inch circle on lightly floured surface. Line 9-inch pie plate with dough; flute edge.

2 Beat butter in large bowl with electric mixer at medium speed about 2 minutes or until creamy. Add sugar; beat 3 minutes or until light and fluffy. Add eggs, one at a time, beating well after each addition. Add corn syrup, bourbon, vanilla and salt; beat until well blended. Pour into crust; arrange pecans on top.

3 Bake on lowest rack of oven 50 to 55 minutes or until knife inserted near center comes out clean. (Filling will be puffy.) Cool completely on wire rack. Serve at room temperature or cover and refrigerate up to 24 hours.

> **Tip:** Use your favorite recipe for pie dough or the Single-Crust Pie Dough on page 11. Or use a refrigerated pie crust (half of a 14-ounce package) or a frozen 9-inch pie crust. Prepare the filling and bake as directed.

Decadent Brownie Pie

makes 12 servings

12 ounces bittersweet chocolate chopped

½ cup (1 stick) butter

2 eggs

½ cup sugar

1 cup all-purpose flour

½ teaspoon salt

Vanilla ice cream

Hot fudge topping, heated

Maraschino cherries (optional)

1 Preheat oven to 350°F. Grease 10-inch tart pan with removable bottom or 9-inch square baking pan. Combine chocolate and butter in small saucepan; heat over low heat until melted, stirring frequently.

2 Beat eggs in medium bowl with electric mixer at medium speed 30 seconds. Gradually add sugar; beat 1 minute. Beat in chocolate mixture, scraping down side of bowl once. Beat in flour and salt at low speed just until blended. Spread in prepared pan.

3 Bake 25 minutes or just until center is set. Cool completely in pan on wire rack. Cut into wedges; top with ice cream, hot fudge topping and cherry, if desired.

Shortcut Apple Raisin Pie

makes 8 servings

2 cans (21 ounces each) apple pie filling

1 cup raisins

½ teaspoon ground ginger, divided

1 unbaked 9-inch pie crust

¼ cup all-purpose flour

¼ cup packed brown sugar

2 tablespoons butter, melted

¾ cup chopped walnuts

1 Preheat oven to 375°F.

2 Combine pie filling, raisins and ¼ teaspoon ginger in large bowl; mix well. Pour into crust.

3 Combine flour, brown sugar and remaining ¼ teaspoon ginger in small bowl; stir in butter until crumbly. Stir in walnuts; sprinkle over filling.

4 Bake 35 to 45 minutes or until topping is golden.

Maple Pumpkin Pie

makes 8 servings

1 refrigerated pie crust (half of 14-ounce package)

1 can (15 ounces) pure pumpkin

1 can (12 ounces) evaporated milk

2 eggs

⅓ cup sugar

⅓ cup maple syrup, plus additional for garnish

1 teaspoon ground cinnamon, plus additional for garnish

½ teaspoon ground ginger

½ teaspoon salt

Whipped cream (optional)

Additional maple syrup (optional)

1 Let crust stand at room temperature 15 minutes. Preheat oven to 425°F.

2 Line 9-inch deep-dish pie plate with crust; flute or crimp edge.

3 Whisk pumpkin, evaporated milk, eggs, sugar, ⅓ cup maple syrup, 1 teaspoon cinnamon, ginger and salt in large bowl until well blended. Pour into crust.

4 Bake 15 minutes. *Reduce oven temperature to 350°F.* Bake 40 minutes or until center is set. Cool on wire rack. Let stand at least 30 minutes before serving. Serve pie warm, at room temperature or chilled. Garnish with whipped cream, additional maple syrup and cinnamon.

Cool & Creamy

Crunchy Ice Cream Pie
makes 6 servings

8 ounces semisweet chocolate, chopped

2 tablespoons butter

1½ cups crisp rice cereal

½ gallon chocolate chip or fudge ripple ice cream, softened

Hot fudge topping

1 Spray 9-inch pie plate with nonstick cooking spray.

2 Combine chocolate and butter in large saucepan; heat over low heat until melted, stirring frequently.

3 Remove from heat; stir in cereal until well blended. Spoon mixture into prepared pie plate; press into bottom and 1 inch up side to form crust.

4 Spread ice cream evenly in crust. Cover and freeze until ready to serve. Let pie stand at room temperature 10 minutes before serving. Drizzle with hot fudge topping.

Banana Cream Pie

makes 8 servings

1 refrigerated pie crust (half of 14-ounce package), at room temperature

⅔ cup sugar

¼ cup cornstarch

¼ teaspoon salt

2½ cups milk

4 egg yolks, beaten

2 tablespoons butter, softened

2 teaspoons vanilla

2 medium bananas

1 teaspoon lemon juice

Whipped cream and toasted sliced almonds (optional)

1 Preheat oven to 400°F. Line 9-inch pie plate with crust; flute edge. Prick bottom and side all over with fork. Bake 10 minutes or until crust is golden brown. Cool completely on wire rack.

2 Combine sugar, cornstarch and salt in medium saucepan; whisk in milk until well blended. Cook over medium heat about 12 minutes or until mixture boils and thickens, stirring constantly. Boil 2 minutes, stirring constantly. Remove from heat.

3 Gradually whisk ½ cup hot milk mixture into egg yolks in small bowl. Gradually whisk mixture back into milk mixture in saucepan. Cook over medium heat about 5 minutes, whisking constantly. Remove from heat; whisk in butter and vanilla. Cool 20 minutes, stirring occasionally. Strain through fine-mesh strainer into medium bowl. Press plastic wrap onto surface of pudding; cool about 30 minutes or until lukewarm.

4 Cut bananas into ¼-inch slices; toss with lemon juice in medium bowl. Spread half of pudding in cooled crust; arrange bananas over pudding. (Reserve several slices for garnish, if desired.) Spread remaining pudding over bananas. Refrigerate 4 hours or overnight. Garnish with whipped cream, almonds and reserved banana slices.

Chocolate Peanut Butter Pie

makes 8 servings

10 whole chocolate graham crackers, broken into pieces

2 tablespoons granulated sugar

¼ cup (½ stick) butter, melted

1 package (8 ounces) cream cheese, softened

1 cup creamy peanut butter

1¾ cups powdered sugar, divided

3 tablespoons butter, softened

1¾ teaspoons vanilla, divided

¼ teaspoon salt

2 cups cold whipping cream

½ cup unsweetened cocoa powder

2 packages (1½ ounces each) chocolate peanut butter cups, chopped

1 Preheat oven to 350°F. Combine graham crackers and granulated sugar in food processor; process until finely ground. Add ¼ cup melted butter; process until well blended. Press into bottom and up side of 9-inch pie plate.

2 Bake crust 8 minutes. Cool completely on wire rack.

3 Meanwhile, beat cream cheese, peanut butter, ¾ cup powdered sugar, 3 tablespoons softened butter, 1 teaspoon vanilla and salt in large bowl with electric mixer at medium speed about 3 minutes or until light and fluffy. Spread filling in cooled crust; smooth top. Refrigerate pie while preparing topping.

4 Beat cream, remaining 1 cup powdered sugar, ¾ teaspoon vanilla and cocoa in medium bowl with electric mixer at high speed 1 to 2 minutes or until soft peaks form. Spread chocolate whipped cream over peanut butter layer; sprinkle with peanut butter cups. Refrigerate several hours or overnight.

Coconut Meringue Pie

makes 8 servings

1¼ cups sugar, divided

½ cup self-rising flour

1¼ cups milk

3 eggs, separated

2 tablespoons butter

1 teaspoon vanilla

1¼ cups flaked coconut, divided

1 baked 9-inch pie crust

1 Preheat oven to 350°F.

2 Combine 1 cup sugar and flour in medium saucepan; mix well. Whisk in milk, egg yolks, butter and vanilla until well blended; cook over medium heat until mixture thickens, whisking constantly. Remove from heat; stir in 1 cup coconut. Pour into baked crust.

3 Beat egg whites in medium bowl with electric mixer at high speed until foamy. Gradually add remaining ¼ cup sugar, beating until soft peaks form. Spread meringue over filling; sprinkle with remaining ¼ cup coconut.

4 Bake 10 to 15 minutes or until meringue is golden brown. Cool completely on wire rack.

Easy Cherry Cream Pie

makes 8 servings

- 1 pint vanilla ice cream, softened
- ½ (16-ounce) package frozen dark sweet cherries, chopped
- 1 cup whipping cream
- 1 tablespoon powdered sugar
- ⅛ teaspoon almond extract
- 1 (6-ounce) graham cracker or chocolate crumb pie crust

1 Combine ice cream and cherries in large bowl; stir just until blended.

2 Beat cream, powdered sugar and almond extract in medium bowl with electric mixer at medium-high speed until soft peaks form.

3 Spread ice cream evenly in crust. Spread whipped cream over ice cream; freeze 1 hour or until firm. Let stand at room temperature 10 minutes before serving.

Chocolate Velvet Pie

makes 8 servings

1 frozen 9-inch deep-dish
    pie crust
4 ounces semisweet
    chocolate
¾ cup half-and-half
3 eggs, divided
1 egg yolk
10 tablespoons sugar,
    divided
1 teaspoon vanilla, divided
⅛ teaspoon salt
1 package (8 ounces)
    cream cheese, softened
¼ cup whipping cream
    Fresh raspberries and
    chocolate curls
    (optional)

1 Preheat oven to 400°F. Prick holes in bottom of crust with fork. Bake 10 minutes or until lightly browned. Cool completely on wire rack. *Reduce oven temperature to 350°F.*

2 Combine chocolate and half-and-half in medium saucepan; heat over medium-low heat until chocolate is melted and mixture is smooth, stirring frequently. Remove from heat.

3 Beat 2 eggs and egg yolk in small bowl until blended. Add to chocolate mixture; whisk until blended. Add 6 tablespoons sugar, ½ teaspoon vanilla and salt; whisk until well blended. Spread evenly in crust.

4 Beat cream cheese and remaining 4 tablespoons sugar in medium bowl with electric mixer at medium-high speed until smooth. Beat in cream, remaining egg and ½ teaspoon vanilla until well blended. Gently spread cream cheese mixture over chocolate filling, covering completely.

5 Bake 40 minutes or until set. Cool completely on wire rack. Cover and refrigerate at least 2 hours before serving. Garnish with raspberries and chocolate curls.

Summer Berry Custard Pie

makes 8 servings

9 whole graham crackers

2 eggs, divided

2 tablespoons butter, melted and cooled

1 cup milk

½ cup sugar

3 tablespoons cornstarch
   Pinch of salt

1½ cups plain Greek yogurt

2 teaspoons vanilla

1½ cups fresh blueberries, raspberries or a combination

1 Preheat oven to 350°F. Spray 9-inch glass pie plate with nonstick cooking spray.

2 Place graham crackers in food processor; process until finely ground. Transfer to medium bowl; stir in 1 egg and butter until well blended. Press mixture into bottom and up side of prepared pie plate.

3 Bake crust 10 minutes. Cool completely on wire rack.

4 Combine milk, remaining egg, sugar, cornstarch and salt in medium saucepan; cook over medium heat 5 to 8 minutes or until mixture comes to a boil and thickens, whisking constantly. Remove from heat; stir in yogurt and vanilla.

5 Pour filling into crust; press plastic wrap directly onto surface of filling. Refrigerate 4 hours or until firm. Top with berries just before serving.

Snickery Pie

makes 8 to 10 servings

Crust

1½ cups vanilla wafer cookie crumbs

3 tablespoons sugar

2 tablespoons unsweetened cocoa powder

¼ cup (½ stick) butter, melted

Filling

2 cups whipping cream

1 package (8 ounces) cream cheese, softened

¾ cup dulce de leche

¼ cup sugar

1 teaspoon vanilla

2 chocolate-covered peanut-nougat-caramel candy bars (1.86 ounces each), finely chopped

Topping

¼ cup dulce de leche

3 tablespoons milk

½ cup semisweet chocolate chips

1½ teaspoons coconut oil

2 chocolate-covered peanut-nougat-caramel candy bars (1.86 ounces each), coarsely chopped

¼ cup chopped salted peanuts

1 For crust, preheat oven to 350°F. Combine cookie crumbs, 3 tablespoons sugar and cocoa in medium bowl; stir in butter until well blended. Press into bottom and up side of 9-inch deep-dish pie plate. Bake 8 minutes. Cool completely on wire rack.

2 For filling, beat 2 cups cream in large bowl with electric mixer at medium-high speed 1 minute or until stiff peaks form. Transfer to medium bowl. (Do not wash out mixer bowl.)

3 Combine cream cheese, ¾ cup dulce de leche, ¼ cup sugar and vanilla in same large bowl; beat at medium speed 1 to 2 minutes or until well blended, scraping bowl and beater once.

4 Gently fold in whipped cream in three additions until well blended (no streaks of white remain). Fold in finely chopped candy bars. Spread evenly in prepared crust. Refrigerate 4 hours or overnight.

5 For topping, microwave ¼ cup dulce de leche in small bowl on HIGH 20 seconds. Stir; microwave 10 seconds or until softened. Stir in milk until well blended. Combine chocolate and coconut oil in small saucepan; heat over low heat until chocolate is melted and mixture is smooth, stirring frequently. Sprinkle coarsely chopped candy bars and peanuts over top of pie; drizzle with dulce de leche and chocolate mixtures. Refrigerate until topping is set.

Maple Sweet Potato Cheesecake Pies

makes 12 servings

1 package (8 ounces) cream cheese, softened

½ cup vanilla yogurt

1 can (16 ounces) sweet potatoes, drained and mashed (see Tip)

½ cup pure maple syrup

1 teaspoon vanilla

½ teaspoon ground cinnamon

¼ teaspoon ground cloves

1 egg

1 egg white

12 mini graham cracker crusts

12 pecan halves

1 Preheat oven to 350°F. Beat cream cheese in large bowl with electric mixer at medium speed until creamy. Beat in yogurt until smooth. Add mashed sweet potatoes, maple syrup, vanilla, cinnamon and cloves; beat until smooth. Beat in egg and egg white until well blended.

2 Spoon about ⅓ cup sweet potato mixture into each crust; top with pecan half. Place filled crusts on large baking sheet.

3 Bake 30 to 35 minutes or until set and knife inserted into centers comes out clean. Cool on wire rack 1 hour. Refrigerate before serving.

> **Tip:** Mashing sweet potatoes by hand produces pie filling with a somewhat coarse texture. For a smoother texture, process sweet potatoes in a food processor.

> **Variation:** To make one larger pie instead of individual pies, pour the sweet potato mixture into a 6-ounce graham cracker crust. Bake 40 to 45 minutes or until a knife inserted into the center comes out clean.

Chilly Lemon Pie

makes 8 servings

1¼ cups graham cracker
　　crumbs (about
　　1 package)

¼ cup (½ stick) butter,
　　melted

1 tablespoon sugar

1 tablespoon plus
　　1 teaspoon grated
　　lemon peel, divided

1 can (14 ounces)
　　sweetened condensed
　　milk

½ cup lemon juice
　　(about 3 lemons)

Lemon slices and fresh
　　raspberries (optional)

1 Preheat oven to 350°F. Combine graham cracker crumbs, butter, sugar and 1 teaspoon lemon peel in medium bowl; mix well. Press into bottom and up side of 9-inch pie plate.

2 Bake crust 7 to 10 minutes or until golden brown. Cool completely on wire rack.

3 Whisk sweetened condensed milk, lemon juice and remaining 1 tablespoon lemon peel in medium bowl until well blended. Pour into crust.

4 Cover and refrigerate 3 hours or until set. Garnish with lemon slices and raspberries.

Pistachio Ice Cream Pie

makes 8 servings

1 jar (12 ounces) hot fudge ice cream topping, divided

1 (6-ounce) chocolate crumb pie crust

2 pints pistachio ice cream, softened

½ cup chopped pistachio nuts

1 Spread half of hot fudge topping over bottom of pie crust; freeze 10 minutes.

2 Spread ice cream evenly over hot fudge topping; sprinkle with chopped pistachios. Cover and freeze 2 hours or until firm.

3 Let pie stand at room temperature 10 minutes before serving. Heat remaining hot fudge topping according to package directions; serve with pie.

Chocolate Caramel Pie

makes 10 servings

1½ cups plus 6 tablespoons whipping cream, divided

8 ounces semisweet chocolate, chopped, divided

1 (6-ounce) chocolate crumb pie crust

¼ cup caramel ice cream topping

6 tablespoons sugar, divided

¼ teaspoon salt

3 egg yolks

½ teaspoon vanilla

Whipped topping and caramels (optional)

1 Combine ½ cup cream and 4 ounces chocolate in small saucepan; heat over low heat until chocolate is melted and mixture is smooth, stirring frequently. Set aside to cool slightly. Spread evenly in crust; refrigerate 30 minutes.

2 Spread caramel topping over chocolate; refrigerate 30 minutes.

3 Combine 1 cup cream and remaining 4 ounces chocolate in same saucepan; heat over low heat until chocolate is melted and mixture is smooth, stirring frequently. Stir in 4 tablespoons sugar and salt until well blended. Set aside to cool slightly.

4 Beat egg yolks in small bowl. Pour ½ cup chocolate mixture into egg yolks, whisking constantly. Pour egg mixture back into saucepan; cook and stir over low heat until thickened. Cook 1 minute. (Mixture should reach 160°F.) Transfer to large bowl; stir in vanilla. Refrigerate 30 minutes, stirring occasionally.

5 Beat remaining 6 tablespoons cream and 2 tablespoons sugar in small bowl with electric mixer at high speed until stiff peaks form. Fold whipped cream into chocolate mixture. Gently spread over caramel layer; refrigerate 4 hours or overnight. Garnish with whipped topping and caramels.

Key Lime Pie

makes 8 servings

12 whole graham crackers*

⅓ cup butter, melted

3 tablespoons sugar

2 cans (14 ounces each)
   sweetened condensed
   milk

¾ cup key lime juice

6 egg yolks

Pinch salt

Whipped cream
(optional)

Lime slices (optional)

*Or substitute 1½ cups
graham cracker crumbs.*

1 Preheat oven to 350°F. Spray 9-inch pie plate or springform pan with nonstick cooking spray.

2 Place graham crackers in food processor; pulse until coarse crumbs form. Add butter and sugar; pulse until well blended. Press mixture into bottom and 1 inch up side of prepared pie plate.

3 Bake crust 8 minutes or until lightly browned. Remove to wire rack to cool 10 minutes. *Reduce oven temperature to 325°F.*

4 Meanwhile, beat sweetened condensed milk, lime juice, egg yolks and salt in large bowl with electric mixer at medium-low speed 1 minute or until well blended and smooth. Pour into crust.

5 Bake 20 minutes or until top of pie is set. Cool completely on wire rack. Cover and refrigerate 2 hours or overnight. Garnish with whipped cream and lime slices.

Candy Ice Cream Pie

makes 10 servings

Brown Sugar Crumb
  Crust (recipe follows)

2 cups vanilla ice cream

½ cup chocolate sauce,
  divided

8 snack-size chocolate
  candy bars,* chopped,
  divided

2 cups chocolate ice cream

¾ cup whipping cream,
  whipped

*Use your favorite leftover
candy bars.*

1 Prepare Brown Sugar Crumb Crust.

2 Let vanilla ice cream stand at room temperature about 5 minutes or just until softened; spread evenly over crust. Drizzle with ¼ cup chocolate sauce; sprinkle with half of chopped candy bars. Freeze 1½ hours or until firm.

3 Let chocolate ice cream stand at room temperature about 5 minutes or just until softened; spread evenly over chopped candy bars. Drizzle with remaining ¼ cup chocolate sauce. Freeze 6 hours or until firm.

4 Let pie stand in refrigerator 20 minutes to soften before serving. Spread whipped cream over pie; sprinkle with remaining chopped candy bars.

Brown Sugar Crumb Crust: Preheat oven to 350°F. Combine 1¼ cups graham cracker crumbs, 2 tablespoons packed brown sugar and ⅓ cup melted butter in large bowl; mix well. Press into bottom and up side of 9-inch pie plate. Bake 8 to 10 minutes or until edges are golden brown. Cool completely on wire rack.

Lemon Meringue Pie

makes 8 servings

1 frozen 9-inch deep-dish
   pie crust

1 cup plus 6 tablespoons
   sugar, divided

1 cup lemon juice (from
   about 5 lemons)

6 egg yolks

2 tablespoons grated
   lemon peel

1 tablespoon cornstarch

¼ teaspoon plus pinch of
   salt, divided

½ cup (1 stick) butter,
   cubed

4 egg whites

½ teaspoon cream of tartar

1 Preheat oven to 400°F. Prick holes in bottom of crust with fork. Bake 10 minutes or until lightly browned. Cool completely on wire rack. *Reduce oven temperature to 325°F.*

2 Whisk 1 cup sugar, lemon juice, egg yolks, lemon peel, cornstarch and ¼ teaspoon salt in medium saucepan until well blended. Add butter; cook over medium heat 6 to 8 minutes or until mixture is thick, whisking constantly. Strain through fine-mesh strainer into crust.

3 Beat egg whites and cream of tartar in large bowl with electric mixer at medium-high speed until frothy. Gradually add remaining 6 tablespoons sugar and pinch of salt; beat about 3 minutes or until stiff peaks form. Spread meringue over top of pie.

4 Bake 20 minutes or until meringue is golden brown. Cool completely on wire rack. Refrigerate until ready to serve.

French Silk Pie

makes 8 servings

1 frozen 9-inch deep-dish
   pie crust

1⅓ cups granulated sugar

¾ cup (1½ sticks) butter,
   softened

4 ounces unsweetened
   chocolate, melted

1½ tablespoons unsweetened
   cocoa powder

1 teaspoon vanilla

⅛ teaspoon salt

4 pasteurized eggs*

1 cup whipping cream

2 tablespoons powdered
   sugar

   Chocolate curls (optional)

*The eggs in this recipe are not
cooked, so use pasteurized eggs
to ensure food safety.*

1 Bake pie crust according to package directions. Cool completely on wire rack.

2 Beat granulated sugar and butter in large bowl with electric mixer at medium speed 4 minutes or until light and fluffy. Add melted chocolate, cocoa, vanilla and salt; beat until well blended. Add eggs, one at a time, beating 4 minutes after each addition and scraping down side of bowl occasionally.

3 Pour filling into cooled crust. Refrigerate at least 3 hours or overnight.

4 Beat cream and powdered sugar in medium bowl with electric mixer at high speed until soft peaks form. Pipe or spread whipped cream over chocolate layer; garnish with chocolate curls.

Spiced Raisin Custard Pie

makes 12 servings

1½ cups raisins

½ cup plus 1 teaspoon sugar, divided

3 teaspoons ground cinnamon, divided

1 can (14 ounces) sweetened condensed milk

1 cup biscuit baking mix

1 cup applesauce

3 eggs

¼ cup (½ stick) butter, melted

2 teaspoons vanilla

1 teaspoon ground nutmeg

Whipped cream (optional)

1 Preheat oven to 325°F. Spray 10-inch glass pie plate with nonstick cooking spray.

2 Place raisins in medium bowl. Combine 1 teaspoon sugar and 1 teaspoon cinnamon in small bowl; reserve half for top of pie. Sprinkle remaining cinnamon-sugar over raisins; toss to coat.

3 Combine remaining ½ cup sugar and 2 teaspoons cinnamon, sweetened condensed milk, baking mix, applesauce, eggs, butter, vanilla and nutmeg in large bowl; beat with electric mixer at medium speed 2 minutes or until well blended. Pour into prepared pie plate.

4 Bake 10 minutes. Remove from oven; top with spiced raisins and sprinkle with reserved cinnamon-sugar. Bake 35 to 40 minutes (center will be soft). Cool to room temperature on wire rack; refrigerate at least 2 hours before serving. Top with whipped cream, if desired.

Amaretto Coconut Cream Pie

makes 8 servings

¼ cup flaked coconut

1 container (8 ounces) whipped topping, divided

1 container (6 ounces) coconut or vanilla yogurt

¼ cup amaretto liqueur

1 package (4-serving size) coconut instant pudding and pie filling mix

1 (6-ounce) graham cracker pie crust

Fresh strawberries and mint leaves (optional)

1 Place coconut in small skillet; cook and stir over medium heat about 2 minutes or until lightly browned. Remove to small bowl; cool completely.

2 Whisk 2 cups whipped topping, yogurt and amaretto in large bowl until blended. Add pudding mix; whisk 2 minutes or until thickened.

3 Spread mixture evenly in crust; spread remaining whipped topping over filling. Sprinkle with toasted coconut. Refrigerate until ready to serve. Garnish with strawberries and mint.

Mexican Ice Cream Pie

makes 6 to 8 servings

- 1 cup butter pecan ice cream, softened
- 1 (6-ounce) chocolate crumb pie crust
- ½ cup caramel ice cream topping
- 2 cups coffee ice cream, softened
- 1 jar (12 ounces) hot fudge ice cream topping
- ½ cup coffee liqueur (optional)

1 Spread butter pecan ice cream evenly in crust. Freeze 20 minutes or until almost firm.

2 Spread caramel topping over butter pecan ice cream. Freeze 20 minutes or until firm.

3 Spread coffee ice cream over caramel topping. Freeze pie 6 hours or overnight.

4 Combine hot fudge topping and coffee liqueur, if desired, in small saucepan; cook and stir over medium heat until heated through.

5 Let pie stand at room temperature 10 minutes before serving. Drizzle with hot fudge mixture.

Sweet & Simple

Swedish Apple Pie

makes 8 servings

4 **Granny Smith apples, peeled and thinly sliced**

1 **cup plus 1 tablespoon sugar, divided**

1 **tablespoon ground cinnamon**

¾ **cup (1½ sticks) butter, melted**

1 **cup all-purpose flour**

½ **cup chopped nuts**

2 **eggs**

¼ **teaspoon salt**

1 Preheat oven to 350°F.

2 Spread apples in 9-inch deep-dish pie plate or 9-inch square baking dish. Combine 1 tablespoon sugar and cinnamon in small bowl; sprinkle over apples. Drizzle with butter.

3 Combine remaining 1 cup sugar, flour, nuts, eggs and salt in medium bowl; mix well. (Mixture will be thick.) Spread batter over apples.

4 Bake 50 to 55 minutes or until top is golden brown.

Chocolate Chess Pie

makes 8 servings

4 ounces unsweetened
   chocolate, chopped

3 tablespoons butter

3 eggs

1 egg yolk

1¼ cups sugar

½ cup half-and-half

1 to 2 teaspoons instant
   coffee granules

¼ teaspoon salt

1 unbaked 9-inch pie crust

   Whipped cream

   Chocolate-covered coffee
   beans (optional)

1 Preheat oven to 325°F.

2 Combine chocolate and butter in small saucepan; heat over low heat until melted, stirring frequently. Set aside to cool 15 minutes.

3 Whisk eggs and egg yolk in medium bowl. Whisk in sugar, half-and-half, coffee granules and salt until blended. Whisk in chocolate mixture until smooth. Pour into crust.

4 Bake 35 minutes or until set. Cool completely on wire rack. Refrigerate 2 hours or until ready to serve. Top with whipped cream; garnish with chocolate-covered coffee beans.

Note: Use 2 teaspoons instant coffee granules for a more pronounced coffee flavor; use a smaller amount if a more subtle coffee flavor is preferred.

Shoofly Pie

makes 8 servings

1 cup all-purpose flour

⅔ cup packed brown sugar

¼ cup (½ stick) plus
   1 tablespoon butter,
   cut into small pieces,
   divided

3 eggs, beaten

½ cup molasses

½ teaspoon baking soda

⅔ cup hot water

1 frozen 9-inch deep-dish
   pie crust

Whipped cream

1 Preheat oven to 325°F. Combine flour and brown sugar in medium bowl; mix well.

2 For topping, remove ½ cup flour mixture to small bowl. Cut in 1 tablespoon butter with pastry blender or fingertips until mixture resembles coarse crumbs.

3 Melt remaining ¼ cup butter; cool slightly. Whisk eggs, molasses and melted butter in large bowl until well blended. Gradually stir in flour mixture. Stir in baking soda. Gradually stir in hot water until blended. Pour into crust; sprinkle with topping.

4 Bake 40 minutes or until filling is puffy and set. Cool completely on wire rack. Serve with whipped cream.

Buttermilk Pie

makes 8 servings

1½ cups sugar

1 tablespoon cornstarch

3 eggs

½ cup buttermilk

¼ cup (½ stick) butter, melted and cooled

1 tablespoon lemon juice

1 teaspoon vanilla

1 (6-ounce) graham cracker pie crust

Whipped cream

1 Preheat oven to 350°F.

2 Combine sugar and cornstarch in medium bowl; mix well. Add eggs, buttermilk, butter, lemon juice and vanilla; beat with electric mixer at medium speed until smooth. Pour into crust.

3 Bake 40 minutes or until set. Cool completely on wire rack. Refrigerate 2 hours or until ready to serve. Serve with whipped cream.

Bourbon-Laced Sweet Potato Pie

makes 8 servings

1 pound sweet potatoes, peeled and cut into 1-inch pieces (about 2 medium)

2 tablespoons butter

¾ cup packed brown sugar

1 teaspoon ground cinnamon, plus additional for garnish

¼ teaspoon salt

2 eggs

¾ cup whipping cream

¼ cup bourbon or whiskey

1 refrigerated pie crust (half of 14-ounce package)

Whipped cream (optional)

1 Place sweet potatoes in large saucepan; add water to cover. Bring to a boil over high heat. Reduce heat to low; simmer 20 minutes or until very tender. Drain sweet potatoes; transfer to large bowl.

2 Let crust stand at room temperature 15 minutes. Preheat oven to 350°F.

3 Add butter to sweet potatoes; beat with electric mixer at medium speed until smooth. Add brown sugar, 1 teaspoon cinnamon and salt; beat until well blended. Add eggs, one at a time, beating well after each addition. Beat in cream and bourbon until blended.

4 Line 9-inch pie plate with crust; flute edge. Pour sweet potato mixture into crust.

5 Bake 50 minutes or until knife inserted near center comes out clean. Remove to wire rack; cool at least 1 hour before serving. Serve warm or at room temperature. Top with whipped cream, if desired; garnish with additional cinnamon.

Tip: The pie can be cooled completely, covered and refrigerated up to 24 hours before serving. Let stand at room temperature at least 30 minutes before serving.

Fancy Fudge Pie

makes 8 servings

1 cup chocolate wafer crumbs

⅓ cup butter, melted

1⅓ cups semisweet chocolate chips

¾ cup packed brown sugar

½ cup (1 stick) butter, softened

3 eggs

1 cup chopped pecans

½ cup all-purpose flour

1 teaspoon vanilla

½ teaspoon instant espresso powder

¼ teaspoon salt

Chocolate syrup (optional)

1 Preheat oven to 375°F. Combine wafer crumbs and ⅓ cup melted butter in small bowl; mix well. Press into bottom and up side of 9-inch pie plate.

2 Bake crust 5 minutes. Cool completely on wire rack.

3 Place chocolate chips in small microwavable bowl; microwave on HIGH 1 minute or until melted, stirring after 30 seconds. Set aside to cool slightly.

4 Beat brown sugar and ½ cup softened butter in large bowl with electric mixer at medium speed until light and fluffy. Add eggs, one at a time, beating well after each addition. Stir in melted chocolate, pecans, flour, vanilla, espresso powder and salt until blended. Pour into crust.

5 Bake 30 minutes or until set. Cool completely on wire rack. Cover and refrigerate 2 hours or until ready to serve. Drizzle with chocolate syrup, if desired.

Warm Mixed Berry Pie

makes 8 servings

1 refrigerated pie crust (half of 14-ounce package)

2 packages (12 ounces each) frozen mixed berries

⅓ cup sugar

3 tablespoons cornstarch

2 teaspoons grated orange peel

¼ teaspoon ground ginger

1 Let crust stand at room temperature 15 minutes. Preheat oven to 350°F.

2 Combine berries, sugar, cornstarch, orange peel and ginger in large bowl; toss gently to coat. Spread in large ovenproof skillet.

3 Roll out crust into 12-inch circle on lightly floured surface. Place crust over fruit mixture; flute edge as desired. Cut several slits in crust.

4 Bake 1 hour or until crust is golden brown. Let stand 1 hour before serving.

Cookie-Crusted Pecan Pie

makes 8 servings

½ (16-ounce) package refrigerated sugar cookie dough

¼ cup all-purpose flour

3 eggs

¾ cup dark corn syrup

¾ cup sugar

1 teaspoon vanilla

¼ teaspoon salt

2 cups chopped pecans

1 Let dough stand at room temperature 15 minutes. Preheat oven to 350°F. Lightly spray 9-inch pie plate with nonstick cooking spray.

2 Beat dough and flour in large bowl with electric mixer at medium speed until well blended. Press dough into bottom and ½ inch up side of prepared pie plate. Crimp edge with fork. Bake 20 minutes.

3 Meanwhile, beat eggs in large bowl. Whisk in corn syrup, sugar, vanilla and salt until well blended. Pour into crust; sprinkle evenly with pecans.

4 Bake 40 to 45 minutes or just until center is set. Cool completely on wire rack.

Sour Cream Squash Pie

makes 8 servings

1 **package (12 ounces) frozen winter squash, thawed and drained**

½ **cup sour cream**

1 **egg**

¼ **cup sugar**

1½ **teaspoons pumpkin pie spice**

½ **teaspoon salt**

½ **teaspoon vanilla**

¾ **cup evaporated milk**

1 **(6-ounce) graham cracker pie crust**

¼ **cup chopped hazelnuts, toasted (optional)***

*To toast hazelnuts, spread on baking sheet. Bake at 350°F 6 to 8 minutes or until lightly browned, stirring occasionally.

1 Preheat oven to 350°F.

2 Whisk squash, sour cream, egg, sugar, pumpkin pie spice, salt and vanilla in large bowl until blended. Whisk in evaporated milk until blended. Pour into crust.

3 Bake 1 hour 10 minutes or until set. Cool completely on wire rack. Sprinkle with hazelnuts just before serving, if desired.

Lemon Chess Pie

makes 8 servings

1 refrigerated pie crust (half of 14-ounce package)

3 eggs

2 egg yolks

1¾ cups sugar

½ cup half-and-half

⅓ cup lemon juice

¼ cup (½ stick) butter, melted

3 tablespoons grated lemon peel, plus additional for garnish

2 tablespoons all-purpose flour

Whipped cream (optional)

1 Let crust stand at room temperature 15 minutes. Preheat oven to 325°F.

2 Line 9-inch pie plate with crust; flute or crimp edge.

3 Beat eggs and egg yolks in large bowl. Whisk in sugar, half-and-half, lemon juice, butter, 3 tablespoons lemon peel and flour until well blended. Pour into crust.

4 Bake 40 minutes or until almost set. Cool completely on wire rack. Refrigerate 2 hours or until ready to serve. Serve with whipped cream, if desired; garnish with additional lemon peel.

Tip: To determine doneness, carefully shake the pie. It is done when only the center 2 inches jiggle.

Raspberry Buttermilk Pie

makes 8 servings

1 frozen 9-inch deep-dish
    pie crust

3 eggs, at room
    temperature

2 tablespoons
    all-purpose flour

1 cup buttermilk

¾ cup plus 2 tablespoons
    sugar

¼ cup (½ stick) butter,
    melted

¼ cup honey

½ teaspoon vanilla

¼ teaspoon salt

1½ cups fresh raspberries (do
    not substitute frozen)

1 Preheat oven to 425°F. Place crust on baking sheet. Bake 5 minutes. (It is not necessary to weigh down crust.) Remove from oven; press down any areas that puff up. *Reduce oven temperature to 350°F.*

2 Whisk eggs and flour in large bowl until blended. Whisk in buttermilk, sugar, butter, honey, vanilla and salt until sugar is dissolved. Gently stir in raspberries. Pour into crust.

3 Bake 30 minutes. If crust browns before filling is set, loosely cover pie with foil. Bake 20 minutes or until knife inserted near center comes out clean. Let stand 30 minutes before serving.

Quick Chocolate Pie

makes 8 servings

1¼ cups sugar

½ cup biscuit baking mix

3 tablespoons unsweetened cocoa powder, plus additional for garnish

2 eggs

2 tablespoons (¼ stick) butter, melted

1½ teaspoons vanilla

Whipped cream and sliced fresh strawberries (optional)

1 Preheat oven to 350°F. Spray 9-inch pie plate with nonstick cooking spray.

2 Combine sugar, baking mix and 3 tablespoons cocoa in large bowl; mix well. Whisk in eggs, butter and vanilla until well blended. Pour into prepared pie plate.

3 Bake 40 minutes or until toothpick inserted into center comes out clean. Top with whipped cream, additional cocoa and strawberries, if desired.

Sweet Potato Pecan Pie

makes 8 servings

1 large sweet potato
  (about 1 pound)

3 eggs, divided

8 tablespoons granulated
  sugar, divided

8 tablespoons packed
  brown sugar, divided

2 tablespoons butter,
  melted, divided

½ teaspoon ground
  cinnamon

½ teaspoon salt, divided

1 frozen 9-inch deep-dish
  pie crust

½ cup dark corn syrup

1½ teaspoons lemon juice

1½ teaspoons vanilla

1 cup pecan halves
  Vanilla ice cream
  (optional)

1 Preheat oven to 350°F. Prick sweet potato all over with fork. Bake 1 hour or until fork-tender; let stand until cool enough to handle. *Reduce oven temperature to 300°F.*

2 Peel sweet potato and place in large bowl of stand mixer.

3 Add 1 egg, 2 tablespoons granulated sugar, 2 tablespoons brown sugar, 1 tablespoon butter, cinnamon and ¼ teaspoon salt; beat at medium speed 5 minutes or until smooth and fluffy. Spread mixture in crust; place in refrigerator.

4 Combine remaining 6 tablespoons granulated sugar, 6 tablespoons brown sugar, 1 tablespoon butter, ¼ teaspoon salt, corn syrup, lemon juice and vanilla in medium bowl; beat with electric mixer at medium speed 5 minutes. Add remaining 2 eggs; beat 5 minutes.

5 Place crust on baking sheet. Spread pecans over sweet potato filling; pour corn syrup mixture evenly over pecans.

6 Bake 1 hour or until center is set and top of pie is deep golden brown. Cool completely on wire rack. Serve with ice cream, if desired.

Creamy Mocha Pie

makes 8 servings

4 ounces semisweet chocolate, chopped

2 cups whipping cream, divided

½ cup plus 1 tablespoon sugar, divided

3 eggs

2 teaspoons instant coffee granules

1 teaspoon vanilla, divided

Pinch of salt

1 (6-ounce) graham cracker pie crust

Chocolate shavings (optional)

1 Place chocolate in small microwavable bowl; microwave on HIGH 1½ minutes or until melted, stirring after 1 minute. Set aside to cool slightly.

2 Combine 1 cup cream and ½ cup sugar in medium saucepan; cook over medium heat until sugar is dissolved, whisking constantly. Beat eggs in small bowl; whisk in ¼ cup cream mixture. Pour egg mixture back into saucepan; cook 4 to 5 minutes or until thickened, whisking constantly. Pour into large bowl.

3 Add melted chocolate, coffee granules, ½ teaspoon vanilla and salt; beat with electric mixer at low speed until blended. Beat at medium speed 2 minutes. Pour into crust. Cool 15 minutes; cover and refrigerate 3 hours or overnight.

4 Beat remaining 1 cup cream in medium bowl with electric mixer at high speed 1 minute. Add remaining 1 tablespoon sugar and ½ teaspoon vanilla; beat until soft peaks form. Top pie with whipped cream; garnish with chocolate shavings.

Apple Buttermilk Pie

makes 8 servings

2 medium Granny Smith apples, peeled and cut into ½-inch pieces

3 eggs

1½ cups sugar, divided

1 cup buttermilk

⅓ cup butter, melted

2 tablespoons all-purpose flour

2 teaspoons vanilla

2 teaspoons ground cinnamon, divided, plus additional for garnish

½ teaspoon ground nutmeg, divided

1 unbaked 9-inch pie crust

Whipped cream (optional)

1 Preheat oven to 350°F. Place apples in medium bowl; cover with cold water and set aside.

2 Beat eggs in medium bowl. Reserve 1 teaspoon sugar in small bowl. Add remaining sugar, buttermilk, butter, flour, vanilla, 1 teaspoon cinnamon and ¼ teaspoon nutmeg to eggs; whisk until well blended.

3 Drain apples well; place in unbaked crust. Pour buttermilk mixture over apples. Add remaining 1 teaspoon cinnamon and ¼ teaspoon nutmeg to reserved sugar in small bowl; sprinkle over top of pie.

4 Bake 50 to 60 minutes or until knife inserted into center comes out clean. Serve warm or at room temperature; garnish with whipped cream and additional cinnamon.

Sweet Potato Pie

makes 8 servings

1 large or 2 medium
  sweet potatoes (1½ to
  2 pounds), peeled and
  cut into 1-inch pieces
½ cup sugar
¼ cup (½ stick) butter
2 eggs
¼ cup buttermilk
½ teaspoon vanilla
1 unbaked 9-inch
  deep-dish pie crust
  Whipped cream and
  ground cinnamon
  (optional)

1 Place potatoes in large saucepan; add water to cover. Bring to a boil; cook 15 to 20 minutes or until potatoes are fork-tender. Drain well.

2 Preheat oven to 375°F. Beat sweet potatoes in large bowl with electric mixer at medium speed until smooth. Add sugar and butter; beat until well blended.

3 Whisk eggs, buttermilk and vanilla in small bowl until well blended. Add to sweet potato mixture; beat until well blended. Pour into crust.

4 Bake 1 hour or until center is set. Cool on wire rack. Garnish with whipped cream and cinnamon.

Cola Pecan Pie

makes 8 servings

1 package (14 ounces)
    refrigerated pie crusts
    (2 crusts)

3 eggs

¾ cup sugar

½ cup corn syrup

¼ cup cola

2 tablespoons butter,
    melted

1½ teaspoons vanilla

¼ teaspoon salt

1½ cups pecan halves

1 Let crusts stand at room temperature 15 minutes. Preheat oven to 350°F.

2 Press one crust into bottom and up side of 9-inch pie plate. Top with remaining crust. Gently press crusts together; fold edges under and crimp.

3 Whisk eggs, sugar, corn syrup, cola, butter, vanilla and salt in large bowl until well blended. Stir in pecans. Pour into crust.

4 Bake 55 minutes or until set. Cool on wire rack 30 minutes. Serve warm or at room temperature.

The Art of the Tart

Lemon Tart

makes 8 to 10 servings

1 refrigerated pie crust
  (half of 14-ounce
  package)
5 eggs
1 tablespoon cornstarch
1 cup sugar
½ cup (1 stick) butter
½ cup lemon juice

1 Let crust stand at room temperature 15 minutes. Position rack in center of oven. Preheat oven to 450°F.

2 Line 9-inch tart pan with crust, pressing to fit securely against side of pan. Trim any excess crust. Prick bottom and side of crust with fork. Bake 9 to 10 minutes or until golden brown. Cool completely on wire rack. *Reduce oven temperature to 350°F.*

3 Meanwhile, whisk eggs and cornstarch in medium bowl until blended. Combine sugar, butter and lemon juice in medium saucepan; cook and stir over medium-low heat just until butter melts. Whisk in egg mixture; cook 8 to 10 minutes or until thickened, stirring constantly. (Do not let mixture come to a boil.) Pour into medium bowl; stir 1 minute or until cooled slightly. Let cool 10 minutes.

4 Pour cooled lemon curd into crust. Bake 25 to 30 minutes or until set. Cool on wire rack.

Rustic Apple Tart

makes 8 servings

Rustic Tart Dough
(page 125)

2 pounds Golden Delicious
apples, peeled and cut
into ½-inch wedges

2 tablespoons lemon juice

½ cup plus 2 tablespoons
sugar, divided

½ cup raisins

2½ tablespoons apple
brandy,* divided

1 teaspoon ground
cinnamon

1 to 2 tablespoons
all-purpose flour

3 tablespoons butter, cut
into 6 to 8 pieces

1 cup apricot jam

Whipped cream
(optional)

*Or substitute any brandy
or cognac.*

1 Prepare Rustic Tart Dough.

2 Preheat oven to 400°F. Combine apples and
lemon juice in large bowl. Add ½ cup sugar, raisins,
2 tablespoons brandy and cinnamon; toss to coat.

3 Place piece of parchment paper on work surface;
sprinkle with flour. Place dough on parchment;
sprinkle lightly with flour. Roll dough into
18×16-inch oval about ¼ inch thick. Transfer
parchment and dough to rimmed baking sheet.

4 Spread apple mixture over center of dough, leaving
2-inch border. Dot apple mixture with butter.
Fold edge of dough in over fruit, overlapping and
pleating as necessary. Press gently to adhere to
filling. Sprinkle edge of dough with remaining
2 tablespoons sugar.

5 Bake 50 to 55 minutes or until apples are tender
and crust is lightly browned. Cool slightly.

6 Meanwhile, strain jam through sieve into small
saucepan; cook and stir over low heat until smooth.
Stir in remaining ½ tablespoon brandy. Brush warm
tart with jam mixture. Serve with whipped cream,
if desired.

Rustic Tart Dough

2 cups all-purpose flour

1 teaspoon sugar

1 teaspoon grated
   lemon peel

½ teaspoon salt

½ teaspoon ground
   cinnamon

½ cup cold shortening, cubed

½ cup (1 stick) cold butter,
   cubed

⅓ cup ice water

1 Combine flour, sugar, lemon peel, salt and cinnamon in food processor; process until blended.

2 Add shortening; pulse until mixture forms pea-sized chunks. Add butter; pulse until mixture resembles coarse crumbs. Add water; pulse just until dough begins to come together. Shape dough into 6-inch disc; wrap in plastic wrap. Refrigerate at least 1 hour or overnight.

Fresh Fruit Tart

makes 8 to 10 servings

Crust

- 2 **whole wheat naan (6 ounces total), torn into large pieces**
- 3 **tablespoons sugar**
- 4 **tablespoons melted butter**

Filling

- 1 **package (8 ounces) cream cheese, softened**
- 3 **tablespoons sugar**
- 1 **tablespoon lemon juice**
- 1 **teaspoon vanilla**

Topping

- 2 **kiwi, peeled and sliced**
  Assorted fresh berries
- 2 **tablespoons apricot jam, warmed**

1 Preheat oven to 350°F. Line baking sheet with parchment paper; place 9-inch tart pan on baking sheet.

2 Place naan in food processor; process until fine crumbs form (about 2 cups). Add 3 tablespoons sugar; pulse to blend. Add butter, pulse about 15 times or until well blended. Press mixture firmly into bottom and up side of tart pan.

3 Bake 25 to 30 minutes until crust is set and golden brown. Cool completely on wire rack.

4 Beat cream cheese, 3 tablespoons sugar, lemon juice and vanilla in medium bowl with electric mixer at medium speed 2 minutes or until creamy. Pour into cooled crust; smooth top with spatula.

5 Arrange kiwi and berries over filling; brush fruit with jam. Refrigerate at least 20 minutes before serving.

Praline Pumpkin Tart

makes 8 servings

1¼ cups all-purpose flour

1 tablespoon granulated sugar

¾ teaspoon salt, divided

¼ cup cold shortening, cubed

¼ cup (½ stick) cold butter, cubed

3 to 4 tablespoons cold water

1 can (15 ounces) pure pumpkin

1 can (12 ounces) evaporated milk

⅔ cup packed brown sugar

2 eggs

1 teaspoon ground cinnamon

½ teaspoon ground ginger

¼ teaspoon ground cloves

Praline Topping (page 129)

1 Combine flour, granulated sugar and ¼ teaspoon salt in large bowl; mix well. Cut in shortening and butter with pastry blender until coarse crumbs form. Sprinkle with water, 1 tablespoon at a time, stirring with fork until mixture holds together. Shape dough into a ball. Wrap in plastic wrap; refrigerate about 1 hour or until chilled.

2 Roll out dough into 13×9-inch rectangle on lightly floured surface. Press into bottom and up sides of 11×7-inch baking dish. Cover with plastic wrap; refrigerate 30 minutes.

3 Preheat oven to 400°F. Prick bottom of crust all over with fork. Top with foil; fill with dried beans, uncooked rice or ceramic pie weights. Bake 10 minutes or until set.

4 Remove baking dish from oven; gently remove foil lining and beans. Bake 5 minutes or until crust is golden brown. Cool completely on wire rack.

5 Whisk pumpkin, evaporated milk, brown sugar, eggs, cinnamon, remaining ½ teaspoon salt, ginger and cloves in large bowl until well blended. Pour into cooled crust. Bake 35 minutes.

6 Meanwhile, prepare Praline Topping. Sprinkle topping over tart. Bake 15 minutes or until knife inserted 1 inch from center comes out clean. Cool completely on wire rack.

Praline Topping: Combine ⅓ cup packed brown sugar, ⅓ cup chopped pecans and ⅓ cup quick oats in small bowl; mix well. Cut in 1 tablespoon butter with pastry blender or mix with fingertips until coarse crumbs form.

Cranberry Pear Galette

makes 8 servings

1 refrigerated pie crust
   (half of 14-ounce
   package)
¼ cup sugar, divided
1 tablespoon plus
   1 teaspoon cornstarch
2 teaspoons ground
   cinnamon or
   apple pie spice
4 cups thinly sliced peeled
   Bartlett pears
¼ cup dried cranberries
1 teaspoon vanilla
¼ teaspoon almond extract
   (optional)
1 egg white
1 tablespoon water

1 Let crust stand at room temperature 15 minutes. Preheat oven to 450°F. Line baking sheet with parchment paper.

2 Reserve 1 teaspoon sugar for topping. Combine remaining sugar, cornstarch and cinnamon in large bowl; mix well. Add pears, cranberries, vanilla and almond extract, if desired; toss to coat.

3 Place crust on prepared baking sheet. Spread pear mixture over crust, leaving 2-inch border. Fold edge of crust in over fruit, overlapping and pleating as necessary.

4 Beat egg white and water in small bowl until well blended. Brush over crust; sprinkle with reserved 1 teaspoon sugar.

5 Bake 25 minutes or until pears are tender and crust is golden brown.* Cool on baking sheet on wire rack 30 minutes. Serve warm or at room temperature.

If edge browns too quickly, cover loosely with foil after 15 minutes of baking.

French Silk Tart

makes 12 servings

1½ cups finely chopped
chocolate sandwich
cookies (about
15 cookies)

⅓ cup butter, melted

1½ cups whipping cream

1¼ cups semisweet chocolate
chips

1 tablespoon unsweetened
Dutch process cocoa
powder*

2 cups thawed frozen
whipped topping

Grated chocolate
(optional)

*Natural unsweetened cocoa
powder may be substituted.
Dutch process cocoa powder
has a stronger flavor and will
give the filling a darker color
after baking.*

1 Combine cookie crumbs and butter in small bowl;
mix well. Press firmly into bottom of 10-inch
springform pan. Refrigerate until ready to fill.

2 Pour cream into medium microwavable bowl;
microwave on HIGH 1 to 1½ minutes or just
until hot and bubbles appear around edge. Add
chocolate chips; stir until melted. Add cocoa; mix
well. Refrigerate 1 hour or until cold and slightly
thickened.

3 Beat chilled chocolate mixture with electric mixer
at medium speed just until soft peaks form. *Do not
overbeat.*

4 Spread chocolate mixture over crust. Spread
whipped topping over chocolate layer. Garnish
with grated chocolate.

Very Berry Tart

makes 8 servings

1 cup all-purpose flour

5 tablespoons Demerara cane sugar,* divided

5 tablespoons cold butter, cubed

¼ teaspoon salt

4 tablespoons ice water, divided

1 teaspoon almond extract

1 cup fresh or frozen sliced peeled peaches

1 cup fresh or frozen blackberries

½ cup fresh or frozen blueberries

1 tablespoon cornstarch

2 teaspoons orange peel

1 egg yolk

2 tablespoons slivered almonds

Or substitute turbinado sugar for the Demerara cane sugar.

1 Combine flour, 2 tablespoons sugar, butter and salt in food processor; process 1 minute or until crumbly. Slowly drizzle in 3 tablespoons water and almond extract; process 30 seconds to 1 minute or until mixture forms a ball. Wrap dough in plastic wrap; refrigerate 1 to 2 hours.

2 Preheat oven to 400°F. Line baking sheet with parchment paper. Roll out dough to ⅛-inch thickness on lightly floured surface; place on prepared baking sheet. Fold in edge of dough about 1 inch.

3 Combine peaches, blackberries, blueberries, remaining 3 tablespoons sugar, cornstarch and orange peel in medium bowl; stir gently to coat. Drain excess liquid. Mound fruit mixture in center of dough.

4 Beat egg yolk and remaining 1 tablespoon water in small bowl; brush over dough. Sprinkle with almonds.

5 Bake 20 to 30 minutes or until crust is lightly browned. Remove to wire rack to cool slightly. Serve warm or at room temperature.

Custard Peach Tart

makes 8 servings

1 cup all-purpose flour

¼ teaspoon plus ⅛ teaspoon salt, divided

4 tablespoons cold butter, cut into pieces

2 to 3 tablespoons cold water

1 egg, separated

2 eggs

3 tablespoons sugar

1 teaspoon vanilla

¼ teaspoon ground nutmeg

1 cup milk

1 package (16 ounces) frozen peach slices, thawed and well drained

1 Preheat oven to 400°F. Combine flour and ¼ teaspoon salt in medium bowl. Cut in butter with pastry blender until mixture resembles coarse crumbs. Stir in 2 tablespoons water just until moistened, adding additional water if necessary to hold together. Shape dough into a disc.

2 Roll out dough into 11-inch circle on lightly floured surface. Press dough into bottom and up side of 9-inch tart pan with removable bottom. Pierce bottom and side of dough with fork.

3 Beat egg white with fork; lightly brush over bottom and side of dough. Place tart pan on baking sheet. Bake crust 10 minutes; cool completely on wire rack.

4 Meanwhile, whisk egg yolk, 2 eggs, sugar, vanilla, nutmeg and remaining ⅛ teaspoon salt in large bowl until blended. Microwave milk in small measuring cup on HIGH 1 minute or until hot. *Do not boil.* Whisk milk into egg mixture until blended. Arrange peach slices in crust; pour egg mixture over peaches.

5 Bake 25 to 27 minutes or until set. Cool to room temperature on wire rack; refrigerate at least 2 hours or until chilled.

Individual Apple Galettes

makes 5 galettes

1 tablespoon butter

4 medium Granny Smith, Crispin or other firm-fleshed apples, peeled and cut into ¾-inch chunks (about 4 cups)

6 tablespoons granulated sugar

½ teaspoon ground cinnamon

⅛ teaspoon salt

2 teaspoons cornstarch

2 teaspoons lemon juice

1 refrigerated pie crust (half of 15-ounce package)

1 egg, beaten

1 tablespoon coarse or granulated sugar

1 Melt butter in medium saucepan over medium heat; stir in apples, granulated sugar, cinnamon and salt. Cook 10 minutes or until apples are tender, stirring occasionally. Drain apples in colander set over medium bowl; pour liquid back into saucepan. Cook over medium-high heat until liquid is slightly syrupy and reduced by half. Stir in cornstarch; cook 1 minute.

2 Combine cooked apples, lemon juice and cornstarch mixture in medium bowl; stir gently to coat. Set aside to cool to room temperature.

3 Let crust stand at room temperature 15 minutes. Preheat oven to 425°F. Line baking sheet with parchment paper.

4 Place crust on work surface; cut out five circles with 4-inch round cookie cutter. Place circles on prepared baking sheet.

5 Divide apples evenly among crust circles, mounding apples in center of each circle and leaving ½-inch border. Fold edges of crust in over fruit, overlapping and pleating as necessary. Press crust gently into fruit to secure. Brush crust lightly with beaten egg; sprinkle with coarse sugar.

6 Bake about 25 minutes or until crusts are golden brown. Cool on wire rack.

Rustic Plum Tart

makes 8 servings

1 refrigerated pie crust
   (half of 14-ounce
   package)
¼ cup (½ stick) plus
   1 tablespoon butter,
   divided
3 cups sliced plums (about
   6 medium, see Tip)
¼ cup granulated sugar
½ cup all-purpose flour
½ cup old-fashioned or
   quick oats
¼ cup packed brown sugar
½ teaspoon ground
   cinnamon
¼ teaspoon salt
1 egg
1 teaspoon water
1 tablespoon chopped
   crystallized ginger

1 Let crust stand at room temperature 15 minutes. Preheat oven to 425°F. Line baking sheet with parchment paper.

2 Melt 1 tablespoon butter in large skillet over high heat. Add plums; cook and stir 3 minutes or until softened. Stir in granulated sugar; cook 1 minute or until juices are thickened. Remove from heat; set aside to cool.

3 Combine flour, oats, brown sugar, cinnamon and salt in medium bowl; mix well. Cut remaining ¼ cup butter into small pieces. Cut butter into flour mixture with pastry blender until mixture resembles coarse crumbs.

4 Beat egg and water in small bowl. Place crust on prepared baking sheet; brush lightly with egg mixture. Sprinkle with ¼ cup oat mixture, leaving 1½-inch border around edge of crust. Spoon plums over oat mixture, leaving juices in skillet. Sprinkle with ginger. Fold edge of dough in over fruit, overlapping and pleating as necessary. Sprinkle remaining oat mixture over fruit; brush crust with egg mixture.

5 Bake 25 minutes or until crust is golden brown. Cool slightly before serving.

> **Tip:** For the best flavor and presentation, choose dark reddish-purple plums for this recipe and cut the fruit into eight wedges to ensure even cooking.

Pear, Dried Cherry and Almond Galette

makes 8 servings

1 refrigerated pie crust
   (half of 14-ounce
   package)
⅓ cup ground almonds
2 Bosc pears, divided
1 tablespoon butter
2 tablespoons white wine
   or water
2 teaspoons sugar, divided
⅓ cup dried cherries
1 tablespoon half-and-half
   or cream
2 tablespoons sliced
   almonds

1 Let crust stand at room temperature 15 minutes. Preheat oven to 450°F. Roll out dough into 15-inch circle on lightly floured surface. Place on baking sheet; refrigerate until ready to use.

2 Toast ground almonds in medium skillet over medium-high heat about 5 minutes or until fragrant and light golden brown, stirring frequently. Remove to small plate to cool.

3 Cut one pear into ¼-inch pieces. Cut remaining pear in half lengthwise, then cut into quarters and thinly slice.

4 Melt butter in medium skillet over medium heat. Add chopped pear; cook about 10 minutes or until translucent, stirring occasionally. Add wine, 1 teaspoon sugar and cherries; cook 2 to 3 minutes or until most of liquid has evaporated and pears are tender, stirring frequently. Set aside to cool slightly.

5 Spread toasted ground almonds over center of crust, leaving 3-inch border. Top with cooked pear mixture. Arrange sliced pear on top. Fold edge of dough in over fruit, overlapping and pleating as necessary. Brush dough with half-and-half; sprinkle with sliced almonds, pressing gently to adhere. Sprinkle with remaining 1 teaspoon sugar.

6 Bake 20 to 22 minutes or until crust is golden brown. Serve warm.

Apple Cranberry Tart

makes 8 servings

1⅓ cups all-purpose flour

¾ cup plus 1 tablespoon sugar, divided

¼ teaspoon salt

2 tablespoons cold butter, cubed

2 tablespoons cold shortening, cubed

4 to 5 tablespoons ice water

½ cup boiling water

⅓ cup dried cranberries

1 teaspoon ground cinnamon

2 tablespoons cornstarch

4 medium baking apples, peeled and thinly sliced

Vanilla ice cream (optional)

1 Combine flour, 1 tablespoon sugar and salt in medium bowl. Cut in shortening and butter with pastry blender until mixture resembles coarse crumbs. Stir in water, 1 tablespoon at a time, until mixture comes together and forms a soft dough. Wrap dough in plastic wrap; refrigerate 30 minutes.

2 Combine boiling water and cranberries in small bowl; let stand 20 minutes or until softened.

3 Preheat oven to 425°F. Roll out dough into 11-inch circle (about ⅛ inch thick) on lightly floured surface. Press dough into 10-inch tart pan with removable bottom; trim edge of dough even with edge of pan. Prick bottom and side of dough with fork; bake 12 minutes or until crust begins to brown. Cool on wire rack. *Reduce oven temperature to 375°F.*

4 Combine remaining ¾ cup sugar and cinnamon in large bowl; mix well. Reserve 1 teaspoon mixture for topping. Stir cornstarch into remaining mixture. Add apples; toss to coat. Drain cranberries; add to apple mixture and stir to blend.

5 Spread apple mixture in crust; sprinkle with reserved 1 teaspoon sugar mixture. Place tart on baking sheet.

6 Bake 30 to 35 minutes or until apples are tender and crust is golden brown. Cool on wire rack. Serve warm or at room temperature with ice cream, if desired.

Chocolate Walnut Toffee Tart

makes 12 servings

2 **cups all-purpose flour**

1¼ **cups plus 3 tablespoons sugar, divided**

¾ **cup (1½ sticks) cold butter, cubed**

2 **egg yolks**

1¼ **cups whipping cream**

1 **teaspoon ground cinnamon**

2 **teaspoons vanilla**

2 **cups coarsely chopped walnuts**

1¼ **cups semisweet chocolate chips, divided**

1 Preheat oven to 325°F. Line baking sheet with foil.

2 Combine flour and 3 tablespoons sugar in food processor; pulse just until blended. Scatter butter over flour mixture; process 20 seconds. Add egg yolks; process 10 seconds (mixture may be crumbly).

3 Press dough firmly into ungreased 10-inch tart pan with removable bottom or 9- or 10-inch pie plate. Bake 10 minutes or until surface is no longer shiny. Place tart pan on prepared baking sheet. *Increase oven temperature to 375°F.*

4 Combine remaining 1¼ cups sugar, cream and cinnamon in large saucepan; bring to a boil over medium-high heat. Reduce heat to medium-low; simmer 10 minutes, stirring frequently. Remove from heat; stir in vanilla. Sprinkle walnuts and 1 cup chocolate chips evenly over crust. Pour cream mixture over top.

5 Bake 35 to 40 minutes or until filling is bubbly and crust is lightly browned. Cool completely on wire rack.

6 Place remaining ¼ cup chocolate chips in small resealable food storage bag. Microwave on HIGH 20 seconds; knead bag until chocolate is melted. Cut small hole in one corner of bag; drizzle chocolate over tart.

Ginger Plum Tart

makes 6 to 8 servings

1 refrigerated pie crust (half of 14-ounce package)

1¾ pounds plums, cut into ½-inch slices

½ cup plus 1 teaspoon sugar, divided

1½ tablespoons all-purpose flour

1½ teaspoons ground ginger

¼ teaspoon ground cinnamon

⅛ teaspoon salt

1 egg

2 teaspoons water

1 Let crust stand at room temperature 15 minutes. Preheat oven to 400°F.

2 Combine plums, ½ cup sugar, flour, ginger, cinnamon and salt in large bowl; toss to coat.

3 Roll out crust on lightly floured surface into 14-inch circle. Transfer crust to large (10-inch) cast iron skillet. Mound plum mixture in center of crust, leaving 2-inch border around fruit. Fold crust in over fruit, overlapping and pleating as necessary. Gently press crust into fruit to secure.

4 Beat egg and water in small bowl; brush over crust. Sprinkle with remaining 1 teaspoon sugar.*

5 Bake about 45 minutes or until crust is golden brown. Cool on wire rack. Serve warm or at room temperature.

To add sparkle and extra crunch to the tart, use sparkling or coarse sugar to sprinkle on top instead of granulated sugar.

Sour Cream Apple Tart

makes 12 servings

5 tablespoons butter, divided

¾ cup graham cracker crumbs

1¼ teaspoons ground cinnamon, divided

1⅓ cups sour cream

¾ cup sugar, divided

½ cup all-purpose flour, divided

2 eggs

1 teaspoon vanilla

5 cups coarsely chopped peeled Jonathan apples or other firm red-skinned apples

1 Preheat oven to 350°F.

2 Melt 3 tablespoons butter in small saucepan over medium heat. Stir in graham cracker crumbs and ¼ teaspoon cinnamon until well blended. Press crumb mixture into bottom of 9-inch springform pan. Bake 10 minutes. Cool on wire rack.

3 Beat sour cream, ½ cup sugar and 2½ tablespoons flour in large bowl with electric mixer at medium speed until well blended. Beat in eggs and vanilla until well blended. Stir in apples. Spoon into prepared crust.

4 Bake 35 minutes or just until center is set. *Turn oven to broil.*

5 Combine remaining 1 teaspoon cinnamon, ¼ cup sugar and 5½ tablespoons flour in small bowl; mix well. Cut in remaining 2 tablespoons butter with pastry blender or mix with fingertips until mixture resembles coarse crumbs. Sprinkle over top of pie.

6 Broil 3 to 4 minutes or until topping is golden brown. Let stand 15 minutes before serving.

Maple Pecan Tart

makes 8 servings

Crust

1½ **cups all-purpose flour**

½ **cup (1 stick) cold butter, cubed**

3 **tablespoons granulated sugar**

⅛ **teaspoon salt**

3 **tablespoons whipping cream**

1 **egg**

1 **egg yolk**

Filling

¾ **cup packed brown sugar**

¾ **cup maple syrup**

¼ **cup whipping cream**

3 **tablespoons butter**

¼ **teaspoon salt**

4 **egg yolks**

1 **cup chopped pecans**

1 For crust, beat flour, ½ cup butter, granulated sugar and ⅛ teaspoon salt in large bowl with electric mixer at medium speed until mixture resembles coarse crumbs. Beat in 3 tablespoons cream, egg and 1 egg yolk until well blended. Wrap dough in plastic wrap; refrigerate at least 1 hour or up to 3 days.

2 Roll out dough into 10-inch circle (about ¼ inch thick) on lightly floured surface. Press dough into bottom and up side of 9-inch pie plate; trim edge of dough even with edge of pie plate. Cover and refrigerate 30 minutes.

3 Preheat oven to 325°F. For filling, combine brown sugar and maple syrup in small saucepan; cook and stir over medium heat until brown sugar is dissolved. Remove from heat; whisk in ¼ cup cream, 3 tablespoons butter and ¼ teaspoon salt until butter is melted and mixture is smooth. Let stand 5 minutes; whisk in 4 egg yolks and pecans. Pour into crust.

4 Bake 45 to 60 minutes or just until filling is set. Cool on wire rack 1 hour. Cover and refrigerate 30 minutes or until set. Let stand at room temperature 15 minutes before slicing.

Cherry Frangipane Tart

makes 6 to 8 servings

1 refrigerated pie crust
    (half of 14-ounce
    package)
⅔ cup slivered almonds
½ cup all-purpose flour
¼ cup powdered sugar
½ cup (1 stick) butter,
    cubed
2 eggs
1¾ cups pitted frozen
    sweet cherries
    Fresh mint leaves
    (optional)

1 Let crust stand at room temperature 15 minutes. Preheat oven to 450°F. Line 9-inch tart pan with crust; cover with parchment paper. Fill with dried beans or pie weights. Bake 10 minutes. Cool on wire rack; carefully remove parchment paper and beans. *Reduce oven temperature to 350°F.*

2 Combine almonds, flour and powdered sugar in food processor; process until almonds are finely ground. Add butter; pulse to blend. With motor running, add eggs, one at a time; process until blended. Pour into crust; smooth top. Sprinkle with cherries.

3 Bake 35 minutes or until set. Cool completely on wire rack. Garnish with mint.

Blueberry Pear Tart

makes 8 servings

1 refrigerated pie crust
  (half of 14-ounce
  package)
1 medium ripe pear, peeled
  and thinly sliced
8 ounces fresh or thawed
  frozen blueberries
  or blackberries
⅓ cup raspberry fruit spread
½ teaspoon grated fresh
  ginger

1 Let crust stand at room temperature 15 minutes. Preheat oven to 450°F.

2 Spray 9-inch tart pan with nonstick cooking spray. Press crust into bottom and 1 inch up side of pan. Prick crust several times with fork. Bake 12 minutes; cool completely on wire rack.

3 Arrange pear slices in crust; top with blueberries. Place fruit spread in small microwavable bowl; cover and microwave on HIGH 15 seconds. Stir; microwave 5 seconds or until melted. Stir in ginger; let stand 30 seconds to thicken slightly. Pour over fruit in crust. Refrigerate 2 hours before serving.

Apple Galette

makes 6 servings

¾ cup all-purpose flour

¼ cup whole wheat flour

1 teaspoon baking powder

⅛ teaspoon salt

¼ cup (½ stick) cold butter, cubed

3 tablespoons plus 1 teaspoon cold milk, divided

3 cups thinly sliced peeled baking apples

2 tablespoons sugar

1 teaspoon ground cinnamon

1. Preheat oven to 375°F.

2. Combine all-purpose flour, whole wheat flour, baking powder and salt in medium bowl. Cut in butter with pastry blender until mixture resembles coarse crumbs. Add 3 tablespoons milk, 1 tablespoon at a time, mixing with fork until moistened. (Dough will be crumbly.)

3. Turn dough out on lightly floured surface; knead 6 to 8 times or just until dough clings together. Shape dough into a ball.

4. Roll out dough into 12-inch circle on heavy-duty foil. Transfer dough with foil to large baking sheet.

5. Combine apples, sugar and cinnamon in medium bowl; toss to coat. Mound apple mixture in center of dough, leaving 2-inch border. Fold edge of dough in over fruit, overlapping and pleating as necessary. Brush with remaining 1 teaspoon milk. Cover edge of crust with foil.

6. Bake 15 minutes; remove foil. Bake 25 minutes or until crust is golden and apples are tender. Cool on baking sheet 10 minutes. Remove to wire rack; cool 20 minutes. Serve warm.

The Art of the Tart

Savory Pies

Quick Tuna Pies
makes 4 servings

1 container (8 ounces)
    refrigerated crescent
    roll dough
1 can (about 5 ounces)
    water-packed tuna,
    drained
1 tablespoon mayonnaise
1 cup (4 ounces) shredded
    Cheddar cheese

1 Preheat oven to 400°F. Separate dough into triangles; press two perforated triangles together to form four rectangles.

2 Press rectangles into bottoms and up sides of four ovenproof bowls, mugs or ramekins.

3 Combine tuna and mayonnaise in small bowl; mix gently. Spoon tuna mixture evenly over dough; sprinkle with cheese.

4 Bake 10 minutes or until crust is golden brown. Cool slightly before serving.

> **Variations:** Add your favorite vegetables, such as broccoli or peas, to the tuna mixture. Or substitute mozzarella or Swiss cheese for the Cheddar.

Tomato Galette

makes 4 to 6 servings

Crust

  1 cup all-purpose flour
  ½ cup cornmeal
  1 tablespoon sugar
  1 teaspoon minced
      fresh thyme
  ¾ teaspoon salt
  ½ cup (1 stick) cold butter,
      cubed
  ¼ cup ice water

Filling

1½ pounds red, green
      and/or orange
      tomatoes, cut into
      ¼-inch-thick slices
  1 teaspoon salt
  1 cup (4 ounces) shredded
      Asiago, Swiss, Fontina
      or Monterey Jack
      cheese
  ¼ cup grated Parmesan
      cheese
  2 cloves garlic, sliced
      Black pepper
  1 egg
  1 tablespoon whipping
      cream or milk

1 For crust, combine flour, cornmeal, sugar, thyme and ¾ teaspoon salt in medium bowl. Cut in butter with pastry blender or fingertips until mixture resembles coarse crumbs. Sprinkle with water, 1 tablespoon at a time, tossing with fork until mixture holds together. Press dough together to form a ball. Shape dough into a disc; wrap in plastic wrap. Refrigerate at least 2 hours or until firm. (Dough can be made several days in advance.)

2 Preheat oven to 400°F. For filling, combine tomatoes and 1 teaspoon salt in medium bowl; let stand 20 minutes.

3 Line baking sheet with parchment paper. Roll out dough into 14-inch oval on lightly floured surface, pressing together any cracks. Transfer dough to prepared baking sheet.

4 Sprinkle Asiago and Parmesan over dough to within 1 inch of edge. Drain tomatoes; arrange over cheese. Top with garlic and sprinkle with pepper. Fold edge of dough in over tomatoes, tucking ragged ends under, if desired. Beat egg and cream in small bowl; brush over dough.

5 Bake 45 to 50 minutes or until crust is golden brown and tomatoes are lightly browned. Cool slightly; cut into wedges.

Simple Turkey Pot Pie

makes 4 servings

1 tablespoon olive oil

1 cup diced red bell pepper

2 stalks celery, sliced

1 small onion, chopped

2 tablespoons all-purpose flour

1¼ cups chicken broth

1 cup cubed peeled potato

½ teaspoon dried thyme

¾ teaspoon salt, divided

¼ teaspoon black pepper

2 cups cubed cooked turkey

⅓ cup frozen peas

¾ cup all-purpose flour

¾ teaspoon baking powder

⅛ teaspoon baking soda

3 tablespoons cold butter, cut into small pieces

3 to 5 tablespoons buttermilk

1 Preheat oven to 425°F.

2 Heat oil in large skillet over medium heat. Add bell pepper, celery and onion; cook and stir 5 minutes. Stir in flour until blended. Stir in broth, potato, thyme, ½ teaspoon salt and black pepper; bring to a boil. Reduce heat to medium-low; cover and simmer 8 to 10 minutes.

3 Stir in turkey and peas; cook 5 to 7 minutes or until potato is tender and peas are hot. Pour into 1- to 1½-quart casserole.

4 Combine flour, baking powder, baking soda and remaining ¼ teaspoon salt in medium bowl; mix well. Cut in butter with pastry blender until mixture resembles coarse crumbs. Stir in 3 tablespoons buttermilk until dough forms, adding additional buttermilk as needed.

5 Turn out dough onto floured surface; knead lightly. Pat dough to ½-inch thickness; cut out biscuits with 2- to 2½-inch biscuit cutter, rerolling dough as needed. Arrange biscuits over filling.

6 Bake 12 to 14 minutes or until biscuits are lightly browned.

Classic Shepherd's Pie

makes 4 to 6 servings

3 medium russet potatoes (1½ pounds), peeled and cut into 1-inch pieces

½ cup milk

5 tablespoons butter, divided

1 teaspoon salt, divided

½ teaspoon black pepper, divided

2 medium onions, chopped

2 medium carrots, finely chopped

½ teaspoon dried thyme

1½ pounds ground lamb or ground beef

3 tablespoons tomato paste

1 tablespoon Worcestershire sauce

1½ cups reduced-sodium beef broth

½ cup frozen peas

1 Preheat oven to 350°F. Spray 1½-quart baking dish with nonstick cooking spray.

2 Place potatoes in large saucepan; add water to cover by 2 inches. Bring to a boil over medium-high heat; cook 16 to 18 minutes or until tender. Drain potatoes; return to saucepan.

3 Heat milk in small saucepan over medium-high heat until hot. Add 3 tablespoons butter, ½ teaspoon salt and ¼ teaspoon pepper; stir until butter is melted. Pour milk mixture into saucepan with potatoes; mash until smooth. Set aside.

4 Melt remaining 2 tablespoons butter in large skillet over medium heat. Add onions, carrots and thyme; cook 8 to 10 minutes or until vegetables are softened but not browned, stirring occasionally. Add lamb; cook over medium-high heat 4 minutes or until no longer pink. Drain fat. Return skillet to heat; cook 5 to 6 minutes or until lamb is lightly browned. Add tomato paste and Worcestershire sauce; cook 1 minute. Stir in broth; bring to a boil and cook 7 to 8 minutes or until almost evaporated. Stir in peas, remaining ½ teaspoon salt and ¼ teaspoon pepper; cook 30 seconds. Pour into prepared baking dish.

5 Spread mashed potatoes in even layer over lamb mixture; use spatula to swirl potatoes or fork to make crosshatch design on top.

6 Bake about 35 minutes or until filling is hot and bubbly and potatoes begin to brown.

Mushroom Brie Tart

makes 4 servings

Pie dough for 10-inch
   tart pan (see Tip)

2 tablespoons butter

1 package (4 ounces)
   sliced mixed
   mushrooms (oyster,
   shiitake, cremini)

⅓ cup chopped shallots
   or sweet onion

1 tablespoon chopped
   fresh thyme *or*
   1 teaspoon dried thyme

½ teaspoon salt

¼ teaspoon black pepper

3 eggs

½ cup half-and-half
   or whole milk

4 ounces Brie cheese,
   rind removed,
   cut into ¼-inch cubes

1 Preheat oven to 350°F. Press dough into bottom and up side of 10-inch tart pan with removable bottom.

2 Bake crust 10 minutes. Cool on wire rack. *Increase oven temperature to 375°F.*

3 Melt butter in a large skillet over medium heat. Add mushrooms and shallots; cook 5 minutes, stirring occasionally. Stir in thyme, salt and pepper; cook 3 minutes or until mushroom liquid is evaporated. Remove from heat; let stand 5 minutes.

4 Beat eggs in large bowl. Beat in half-and-half until blended. Stir in cheese and mushroom mixture. Pour into crust.

5 Bake 25 to 30 minutes or until center is set and crust is golden brown. Cool on wire rack at least 10 minutes before serving. Serve warm or at room temperature.

Tip: Use your favorite recipe for pie dough or the Single-Crust Pie Dough on page 11. Or use a refrigerated pie crust (half of a 14-ounce package); let stand at room temperature 15 minutes.

Beef Pot Pie

makes 4 to 6 servings

½ cup all-purpose flour

1 teaspoon salt, divided

½ teaspoon black pepper, divided

1½ pounds beef stew meat (1-inch pieces)

2 tablespoons olive oil

1 pound unpeeled new red potatoes, cubed

2 cups baby carrots

1 cup frozen pearl onions, thawed

1 parsnip, peeled and cut into 1-inch pieces

1 cup stout

¾ cup beef broth

1 teaspoon chopped fresh thyme or ½ teaspoon dried thyme

1 refrigerated pie crust (half of 14-ounce package)

1 Preheat oven to 350°F. Combine flour, ½ teaspoon salt and ¼ teaspoon pepper in large resealable food storage bag. Add beef; shake to coat.

2 Heat oil in large skillet over medium-high heat. Add beef; cook until browned on all sides. (Do not crowd beef; cook in batches if necessary.) Transfer to 2½- to 3-quart casserole. Stir in potatoes, carrots, onions and parsnip.

3 Add stout, broth, thyme, remaining ½ teaspoon salt and ¼ teaspoon pepper to same skillet. Bring to a boil, scraping up browned bits from bottom of skillet. Pour over beef and vegetables in casserole; stir to blend.

4 Cover and bake 2½ to 3 hours or until beef is fork-tender, stirring once. Uncover; let stand at room temperature 15 minutes. *Increase oven temperature to 425°F.*

5 Place crust over filling; press edges to seal. Cut several slits in crust to vent. Bake 15 to 20 minutes or until crust is golden brown. Cool slightly before serving.

Crustless Crab-Asparagus Pie

makes 6 servings

4 ounces crabmeat (fresh, frozen or pasteurized)

1½ cups sliced asparagus, cooked

½ cup chopped onion, cooked

1 cup (4 ounces) shredded Monterey Jack cheese

¼ cup grated Parmesan cheese

Black pepper

¾ cup all-purpose flour

¾ teaspoon baking powder

½ teaspoon salt

2 tablespoons butter

1½ cups milk

4 eggs, lightly beaten

1 Preheat oven to 350°F. Spray 10-inch quiche dish or pie plate with nonstick cooking spray.

2 Pick out and discard any shell or cartilage from crabmeat. Layer crabmeat, asparagus and onion in prepared quiche dish; top with cheeses. Season with pepper.

3 Combine flour, baking powder and salt in large bowl; mix well. Cut in butter with pastry blender or two knives until mixture resembles coarse crumbs. Stir in milk and eggs until blended; pour over crabmeat mixture and cheeses.

4 Bake 30 minutes or until puffed and knife inserted near center comes out clean.

Vegetable Tart

makes 8 servings

**Tart Dough
(page 173)**

1 small sweet potato,
    peeled and cut
    crosswise into
    ¼-inch slices
2 tablespoons olive oil,
    divided
¾ teaspoon salt, divided
1 cup sliced mushrooms
½ cup thinly sliced leeks
1 medium zucchini, sliced
1 parsnip, sliced
1 medium red bell pepper,
    cut into 1-inch pieces
8 cloves garlic, minced
1 teaspoon dried basil
½ teaspoon dried rosemary
½ teaspoon black pepper
3 tablespoons grated
    Parmesan cheese
1 egg white, beaten

1 Prepare Tart Dough. Preheat oven to 400°F.
   While dough is resting, prepare vegetables.

2 Spray baking sheet with nonstick cooking spray.
   Place sweet potatoes on baking sheet. Drizzle with
   1 tablespoon oil; sprinkle with ¼ teaspoon salt and
   toss to coat. Spread in single layer; bake 15 to
   20 minutes or until tender, turning once.

3 Heat remaining 1 tablespoon oil in large skillet
   over medium heat. Add mushrooms, leeks,
   zucchini, parsnip, bell pepper, garlic, basil and
   rosemary; cook 8 to 10 minutes or until vegetables
   are tender, stirring occasionally. Season with
   remaining ½ teaspoon salt and black pepper.

4 Roll out dough into 14-inch circle on lightly floured
   surface; transfer to baking sheet or large pizza pan.
   Arrange sweet potato slices evenly over dough,
   leaving 2½-inch border. Spread vegetable mixture
   over sweet potatoes; sprinkle with cheese. Fold
   edge of dough in over vegetables, overlapping and
   pleating as necessary. Brush dough with egg white.

5 Bake 25 minutes or until golden brown. Serve warm.

Tart Dough
makes dough for 1 tart

1 teaspoon active dry yeast
⅓ cup warm water (115°F)
1 egg, beaten
3 tablespoons sour cream
1¼ cups all-purpose flour
¼ cup whole wheat flour
¼ teaspoon salt

1 Dissolve yeast in warm water in medium bowl; let stand 5 minutes or until bubbly. Add egg and sour cream; stir until smooth. Add all-purpose flour, whole wheat flour and salt; stir until soft dough forms.

2 Turn out dough onto lightly floured surface; knead 1 to 2 minutes or until smooth. Shape dough into a ball. Place in large greased bowl; turn to grease top. Cover and let rest in warm place 20 minutes.

Taco Pot Pie

makes 4 to 6 servings

1 pound ground beef

1 package (about 1 ounce) taco seasoning mix

¼ cup water

1 cup canned kidney beans, rinsed and drained

1 cup chopped tomatoes

¾ cup frozen corn, thawed

¾ cup frozen peas, thawed

1½ cups (6 ounces) shredded Cheddar cheese

1 container (about 11 ounces) refrigerated breadstick dough

1 Preheat oven to 400°F. Spray 13×9-inch baking dish with nonstick cooking spray.*

2 Cook beef in large skillet over medium-high heat 6 to 8 minutes or until browned, stirring to break up meat. Drain fat.

3 Add taco seasoning mix and water; cook over medium-low heat 3 minutes or until most liquid is absorbed, stirring occasionally. Stir in beans, tomatoes, corn and peas; cook 3 minutes or until heated through. Remove from heat; stir in cheese. Pour into prepared baking dish.

4 Unwrap breadstick dough; separate into strips. Twist strips; arrange over beef mixture. Press ends of dough against edges of baking dish to secure.

5 Bake 15 minutes or until bread is golden brown and beef mixture is bubbly.

For a one-dish meal, omit the baking dish. Use an ovenproof skillet and arrange the breadstick strips over the beef mixture in the skillet.

Greek Spinach and Feta Pie

makes 6 servings

⅓ cup butter, melted

2 eggs

1 container (15 ounces) ricotta cheese

1 package (10 ounces) frozen chopped spinach, thawed and squeezed dry

1 package (4 ounces) crumbled feta cheese

¾ teaspoon finely grated lemon peel

¼ teaspoon black pepper

⅛ teaspoon ground nutmeg

1 package (16 ounces) frozen phyllo dough, thawed

1 Preheat oven to 350°F. Brush 13×9-inch baking dish lightly with some of butter.

2 Beat eggs in medium bowl. Stir in ricotta, spinach, feta, lemon peel, pepper and nutmeg; mix well.

3 Unwrap phyllo dough; remove eight sheets. Cut phyllo in half crosswise to form 16 rectangles about 13×8½ inches. Cover phyllo with damp cloth or plastic wrap to prevent drying out while assembling pie. Reserve remaining phyllo for another use.

4 Place one piece of phyllo in prepared baking dish; brush top lightly with butter. Layer with another piece of phyllo and brush lightly with butter. Continue layering with six pieces of phyllo, brushing each lightly with butter. Spread spinach mixture evenly over phyllo.

5 Top spinach mixture with piece of phyllo; brush lightly with butter. Repeat layering with remaining seven pieces of phyllo, brushing each piece lightly with butter.

6 Bake 35 to 40 minutes or until golden brown.

Hearty Biscuit-Topped Steak Pie

makes 6 servings

1½ pounds boneless top round steak, cooked and cut into 1-inch pieces

1 package (9 ounces) frozen baby carrots

1 package (9 ounces) frozen peas and pearl onions

1 large baking potato, baked, peeled and cut into ½-inch pieces

1 jar (18 ounces) homestyle brown gravy

½ teaspoon dried thyme

½ teaspoon black pepper

1 container (10 ounces) refrigerated flaky buttermilk biscuit dough

1 Preheat oven to 375°F. Spray 9-inch deep-dish pie plate or 2-quart baking dish with nonstick cooking spray.

2 Combine steak, carrots, peas and onions, potato, gravy, thyme and pepper in large bowl; mix well. Pour into prepared pie plate.

3 Bake 40 minutes. Remove pie from oven; top with biscuits. *Increase oven temperature to 400°F.*

4 Bake 8 to 10 minutes or until biscuits are golden brown.

Variations: This quick pie can be prepared with leftovers of almost any kind. Other steaks, roast beef, stew meat, pork, lamb or chicken can be substituted for the round steak; adjust the gravy flavor to complement the meat. Red potatoes can be used in place of the baking potato, and you can substitute your favorite vegetable combination, such as broccoli, cauliflower and carrots, or broccoli, corn and red peppers for the carrots, peas and onions.

Kale and Caramelized Onion Galette

makes 4 to 6 servings

Crust

1½ cups all-purpose flour

 1 tablespoon sugar

¾ teaspoon salt

½ teaspoon black pepper

½ cup (1 stick) cold butter, cut into pieces

¼ cup ice water

Filling

 3 tablespoons olive oil, divided

 1 large sweet onion, halved and thinly sliced

¾ teaspoon salt, divided

 1 bunch lacinato kale (10 to 12 ounces), stemmed and chopped

 2 cloves garlic, minced

¼ teaspoon black pepper

 1 tablespoon Dijon mustard

 1 cup (4 ounces) shredded Swiss cheese, divided

  Whole or ground nutmeg

 1 egg

 1 tablespoon whipping cream

1 For crust, combine flour, sugar, ¾ teaspoon salt and ½ teaspoon pepper in medium bowl. Add butter; cut in butter with pastry blender or fingers until mixture resembles coarse crumbs. Sprinkle with water, 1 tablespoon at a time, stirring with fork until mixture holds together. Press dough together to form a ball. Shape dough into a disc; wrap in plastic wrap. Refrigerate at least 2 hours or until firm. (Dough can be made several days in advance.)

2 For filling, heat 1 tablespoon oil in medium skillet over medium heat. Add onions; cook 25 to 30 minutes or until golden brown, stirring occasionally and adding water by tablespoonfuls if onions are dry. Stir in ¼ teaspoon salt. Set aside to cool.

3 Meanwhile, place kale in colander; rinse well under cool water. Heat remaining 2 tablespoons oil in large skillet over medium-high heat. Add garlic; cook and stir 1 minute or until garlic is lightly browned. Add kale with water clinging to leaves; cook and stir 5 minutes. Reduce heat to medium; cook and stir 5 minutes or until kale is tender and garlic is golden brown, adding water by tablespoonfuls if kale is dry. Stir in remaining ½ teaspoon salt and ¼ teaspoon pepper. Cool to room temperature.

4 Preheat oven to 400°F. Line baking sheet with parchment paper. Roll out dough into 14-inch circle on lightly floured surface, pressing together any cracks; smooth or trim ragged edges. Transfer

dough to prepared baking sheet. Spread mustard over dough to within 1 inch of edge. Sprinkle with ¾ cup cheese. Top with caramelized onions and kale; sprinkle with remaining ¼ cup cheese. Lightly grate or sprinkle nutmeg over cheese. Fold edge of dough in over vegetables, tucking ragged ends under, if desired. Beat egg and cream in small bowl; brush over dough.

5 Bake 40 minutes or until crust is golden brown and cheese is lightly browned. Cool slightly; cut into wedges.

Lamb and Vegetable Pie

makes 4 to 6 servings

2 tablespoons vegetable oil

1½ pounds boneless leg of lamb, cut into 1-inch pieces

3 medium russet potatoes (about 12 ounces), peeled and cut into 1-inch cubes

16 frozen pearl onions (about 1 cup)

1 cup frozen peas and carrots

3 tablespoons all-purpose flour

1½ cups reduced-sodium beef broth

3 tablespoons chopped fresh parsley

2 tablespoons tomato paste

2 teaspoons Worcestershire sauce

½ teaspoon salt

¼ teaspoon black pepper

1 refrigerated pie crust (half of 14-ounce package)

1 egg, lightly beaten

1 Spray 9-to 10-inch baking dish or deep-dish pie plate with nonstick cooking spray. Heat oil in large saucepan over medium-high heat. Add half of lamb; cook 4 to 5 minutes or until browned, turning occasionally. Remove to plate; repeat with remaining lamb.

2 Add potatoes, onions and peas and carrots to saucepan; cook 2 minutes, stirring occasionally. Stir in lamb and any accumulated juices; cook 2 minutes. Add flour; cook and stir 1 minute. Stir in broth, parsley, tomato paste, Worcestershire sauce, salt and pepper; bring to a boil. Reduce heat to medium-low; cover and simmer about 30 minutes or until lamb and potatoes are tender, stirring occasionally. Transfer to prepared baking dish; let cool 20 minutes.

3 Preheat oven to 400°F. Place pie crust over filling; flute or crimp edge. Brush crust with egg; cut several small slits in top of crust with tip of knife.

4 Bake about 25 minutes or until crust is golden brown and filling is thick and bubbly. Cool 5 minutes before serving.

Sweet Potato Shepherd's Pie

makes 6 servings

1 large sweet potato,
   peeled and cubed
1 large russet potato,
   peeled and cubed
¼ cup milk
¾ teaspoon salt
1 pound ground turkey
2 packages (4 ounces
   each) sliced mixed
   mushrooms *or*
   8 ounces sliced
   cremini mushrooms
1 jar (12 ounces) beef gravy
½ teaspoon dried thyme
¼ teaspoon black pepper
¾ cup frozen peas, thawed

1 Combine sweet potato and russet potato in medium saucepan; add water to cover. Bring to a boil over medium-high heat. Reduce heat to medium-low; cover and simmer 20 minutes or until potatoes are very tender. Drain potatoes; return to saucepan. Mash potatoes with potato masher; stir in milk and salt.

2 Crumble turkey into large ovenproof skillet. Add mushrooms; cook over medium-high heat about 8 minutes or until turkey is no longer pink and mushrooms begin to give off liquid, stirring occasionally. Drain off any excess liquid.

3 Stir in gravy, thyme and pepper; cook over medium heat 5 minutes. Add peas; cook and stir until heated through.

4 Spread mashed potato mixture over turkey mixture; spray with nonstick cooking spray. Preheat broiler.

5 Broil 4 to 5 inches from heat source 5 minutes or until filling is hot and potatoes begin to brown.

Caprese Tartlets

makes 6 tartlets

- 3 **tomatoes, cut into
  4 slices each**
- 3 **tablespoons pesto sauce**
- 1 **sheet frozen puff pastry,
  thawed**
- 6 **ounces fresh mozzarella
  cheese**
- 2 **tablespoons chopped
  kalamata olives**

1 Place tomatoes in large resealable food storage bag. Add pesto; seal bag and turn to coat. Marinate at room temperature 30 minutes.

2 Preheat oven to 425°F. Line baking sheet with parchment paper. Unfold puff pastry on cutting board or work surface. Cut out six 4-inch circles from pastry; place on prepared baking sheet. Top each circle with two tomato slices.

3 Bake 12 minutes or until pastry is puffed and light golden brown. *Turn oven to broil.*

4 Cut cheese into six ¼-inch-thick slices. Top each tart with one cheese slice; broil 1 minute or until cheese is melted. Sprinkle with olives.

Split-Biscuit Chicken Pie

makes 4 to 5 servings

⅓ cup butter

⅓ cup all-purpose flour

2½ cups whole milk

1 tablespoon chicken bouillon granules

½ teaspoon dried thyme

½ teaspoon black pepper

4 cups diced cooked chicken

2 jars (4 ounces each) diced pimientos

1 cup frozen green peas, thawed

1 package (6 ounces) refrigerated biscuits

1 Preheat oven to 350°F. Spray 2-quart casserole or 12×8-inch baking dish with nonstick cooking spray.

2 Melt butter in large skillet over medium heat. Add flour; whisk until blended. Add milk, bouillon, thyme and pepper; whisk until smooth and well blended. Cook and stir until thickened. Remove from heat; stir in chicken, pimientos and peas. Pour into prepared casserole.

3 Bake 30 minutes. Meanwhile, bake biscuits according to package directions.

4 Split biscuits in half; arrange cut sides down over chicken mixture. Bake 3 minutes or until biscuits are heated through.

Metric Conversion Chart

VOLUME MEASUREMENTS (dry)

⅛ teaspoon = 0.5 mL
¼ teaspoon = 1 mL
½ teaspoon = 2 mL
¾ teaspoon = 4 mL
1 teaspoon = 5 mL
1 tablespoon = 15 mL
2 tablespoons = 30 mL
¼ cup = 60 mL
⅓ cup = 75 mL
½ cup = 125 mL
⅔ cup = 150 mL
¾ cup = 175 mL
1 cup = 250 mL
2 cups = 1 pint = 500 mL
3 cups = 750 mL
4 cups = 1 quart = 1 L

VOLUME MEASUREMENTS (fluid)

1 fluid ounce (2 tablespoons) = 30 mL
4 fluid ounces (½ cup) = 125 mL
8 fluid ounces (1 cup) = 250 mL
12 fluid ounces (1½ cups) = 375 mL
16 fluid ounces (2 cups) = 500 mL

WEIGHTS (mass)

½ ounce = 15 g
1 ounce = 30 g
3 ounces = 90 g
4 ounces = 120 g
8 ounces = 225 g
10 ounces = 285 g
12 ounces = 360 g
16 ounces = 1 pound = 450 g

DIMENSIONS

¹⁄₁₆ inch = 2 mm
⅛ inch = 3 mm
¼ inch = 6 mm
½ inch = 1.5 cm
¾ inch = 2 cm
1 inch = 2.5 cm

OVEN TEMPERATURES

250°F = 120°C
275°F = 140°C
300°F = 150°C
325°F = 160°C
350°F = 180°C
375°F = 190°C
400°F = 200°C
425°F = 220°C
450°F = 230°C

BAKING PAN SIZES

Utensil	Size in Inches/Quarts	Metric Volume	Size in Centimeters
Baking or Cake Pan (square or rectangular)	8×8×2	2 L	20×20×5
	9×9×2	2.5 L	23×23×5
	12×8×2	3 L	30×20×5
	13×9×2	3.5 L	33×23×5
Loaf Pan	8×4×3	1.5 L	20×10×7
	9×5×3	2 L	23×13×7
Round Layer Cake Pan	8×1½	1.2 L	20×4
	9×1½	1.5 L	23×4
Pie Plate	8×1¼	750 mL	20×3
	9×1¼	1 L	23×3
Baking Dish or Casserole	1 quart	1 L	—
	1½ quart	1.5 L	—
	2 quart	2 L	—